Lotte Berk   l a vision
long before   say stole)
her

----y wax

Victoria Beckham has embraced a new fitness fad taking Hollywood by storm. The mother of three, who is said to be trying for a baby girl, has been doing four classes a week of the punishing Core Fusion workout. "Beckham was introduced to it by her *Desperate Housewives* pal Eva Longoria and they are now obsessed with it," says a source. "It combines core conditioning with Pilates, the Lotte Berk method designed by a German ballet dancer, interval training and yoga. It's hell!"

– *Daily Mail*, April 2010

Oh, the pain. Oh, the obsession. Oh, the laughs!

– Zoe Wanamaker

For Tracey
Best Wishes

Esther Fairfax

Me, an evening with good friends, 2010.

My

Improper

Mother

and Me

Esther Fairfax

POMONA

A Pomona Book

P-022

Published by Pomona Books 2010
PO Box 50, Hebden Bridge, West Yorkshire HX7 8WA, England, UK
Telephone 01422 846900 · e-mail admin@pomonauk.co.uk

www.pomonauk.co.uk

I

A CIP catalogue record for this book
is available from the British Library

ISBN 978-1-904590-26-2

Set in Monotype Bembo Book
Typeset by Christian Brett

Printed and bound in England by
CPI Cox & Wyman, Reading, RG1 8EX

www.lotte-berk.com

To Michael and Jo
My boys

Acknowledgements

My undying thanks to Jenifer Klepfer who put so much time and effort into getting this manuscript into good shape. Her support and sensitivity was my strength and our friendship made working on this book a good experience. Dear Jen, thank you so much.

I thank my sons Michael and Jo who constantly encouraged me and have given me so much loving support over the years I've tried to write this book.

I also wish to thank Allegra Taylor for valuable suggestions on writing and for encouraging me to believe in myself.

My thanks to Sue Arkell for patiently listening to my first stuttering attempts to make sense of my story.

My deep gratitude to Mark Hodkinson for having the courage to publish my book in the height of a recession.

My thanks to Sue Court for her work as my P.A. and for the enduring friendship that developed.

I am deeply touched and, in gratitude, wish to thank Prue Leith, Zoe Wanamaker and Ruby Wax for their kind and generous contribution to this book. Mother would be thrilled.

Esther Fairfax,
Berkshire, England, May 2010.

Mother sunbathing in our garden, mid-1960s.

It is Easter Bank Holiday Monday. No rush to get up. I make myself a pot of tea and take it on a tray up to bed; there will be at least three cups of tea in the pot. The sun is streaming into my room. I feel its warmth through the comforter. I daydream as I sip my tea. Snapshots of memory unexpectedly fall into my head. Memories I've never bothered to remember; or did I want to forget? One rushes at me. A wave of heat runs up my body and sets my cheeks aflame. It was from 1949. I was 15. I was going out that evening with Derek Roy, a well-known music hall and radio comedian. I had worked with him as his feed in a couple of sketches in summer shows at Bournemouth.

"Will you go down on him?" mother asked as I put on my lipstick.

"I haven't given it a thought," I replied, horrified at the idea.

"Well, if he wants you to, would you? If you do, and swallow it, I'll give you a shilling," mother laughed as she dared me.

His sports car was tiny. But I got my shilling. Ever since, mother called oral sex a 'shilling'.

Mother's irresponsible sense of fun lasted all her life.

Another memory, this one from the 1970s. Mother and I had a weekend to ourselves. I drove her to Pangbourne, a village in Berkshire, where she was going to treat me to a lunch at The George. After lunch we dawdled over coffee. She nudged me, lent close to my ear and whispered:

"Don't look round. There's a man who can't take his eyes off of me. He is a very famous actor, you know." She told me his name.

I lingered, letting my eyes gaze idly around the room until they came to rest on his, quite ugly, face. One of his eyes was a bit smaller than the other and he was not so young. Mother and I had very different taste in men. She was often attracted to quite ugly men or men who were slightly disfigured – not enough to turn her off, but enough to make them different or to evoke her pity.

Eventually he got up and made his way to where we were sitting. Mother put on her most sexy pose, the one she frequently used for photographs. As he came to the table he lent over, putting his face close to mine. In his deep actor's voice he asked me for my telephone number. Out of the corner of my eye I could see my mother's face and whole pose drop.

On another occasion when mother treated me to lunch, as we pulled into Pangbourne I noticed an extremely handsome man with a slight tinge of olive to his complexion and dark, shiny hair. His clothes were most definitely expensive and undoubtedly Italian.

"Wow!" I exclaimed as mother parked her little black Mini. "Just look at that vision." My eyes followed him down the road and into a butcher's shop.

"Go on," mother urged, jabbing me. "Follow him, talk to him."

"No, I can't," I whispered as I struggled with my shyness and desire.

"If you go into the butcher's shop and come out talking to him, you'll find a fiver on your seat."

My heart raced as I went into the butcher's. He was at the till, paying. I had no idea what to say.

"Excuse me," I stuttered. "Please forgive me but my mother bet me that I wouldn't have the courage to speak to you."

Though rather taken aback, he recovered quickly enough to tell me where he lived as we walked out of the shop and towards mother's car. I thanked him. As I opened the door to get in, there on my seat lay a crisp five-pound note. We forgot about the food we were en route to buy and laughed all the way home.

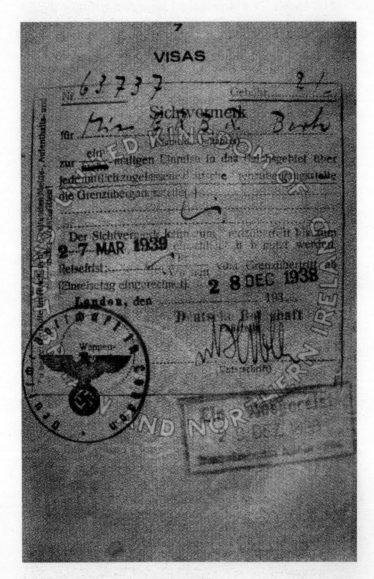

My life saving passport issued in error.

One

1936, Opa & Me in Cologne.
A walk in the park.

Mother's father Nicoli Heymansohn was born in 1897 on a farm in a small village near Riga in Latvia. One of 14, he was brought up strictly following the Jewish faith. As a young man eager to pursue his vocation as a cantor, Nicoli moved to Moscow to start his training. While there, he found a job as a window dresser in a tailor's shop and was keen to learn all aspects of this field. This held him in good stead for his future.

As a series of anti-Semitic pogroms spread destruction and fear through Russia, Nicoli fled to Holland. He again found work in a tailor's shop. On a business trip to Cologne he met Regina, the love of his life. He moved to Cologne to marry her. Regina came from a wealthy family that owned stables in the city centre where shire horses were used to transport food, coal, wood and goods delivered to private homes and businesses throughout the city.

Once settled, Nicoli opened his first tailor's shop and went on to become a successful businessman. They started a family. Hilde was their first-born. Lotte came along 18 months later. They were a happy, conventional family. What went wrong?

"I was a hateful child, a difficult child: ugly, thin and teased at school for my matchstick legs. My black hair was cut short. I was so jealous of Hilde who had thick, long blonde hair that was plaited and hung down her back like a golden rope. She was always sickly with minor ailments and got all the attention from my parents. Hilde was the pretty one, with a sweet smile and demure manner. How things changed when we grew up.

Our apartment was above father's shop. He came up and had lunch with us every day, saying he couldn't go the whole day without seeing his lovely family. As father became more prosperous he bought a large house that straddled two streets in the city centre. The ground floor became a smart tailor's shop. We had a huge apartment on the first floor and father rented out the other apartment. After this he began fulfilling his dreams of owning a chain of tailor's shops all named after mother's maiden name, Müller.

Father's fortune grew. He enjoyed his wealth and wanted only the best for us. He bought a Mercedes-Benz 770K, an ostentatious eight-seater vehicle that was the official car of Kaiser Wilhelm II. On family outings Father drove the Mercedes and Mother trotted behind in her horse and carriage, refusing to sit in such obvious and vulgar extravagance.

Father loved to design our clothes. He, himself, was always dressed immaculately and smelled deliciously of aftershave. He glowed with pride driving down the street with his two daughters. In the summer he insisted we wear our blue capes and muff, in winter we had ones of white fur. He designed them all. Our new apartment was palatial with marble pillars and servants' quarters although we only had one live-in maid. The cook and cleaner came in daily.

I know I was spoiled and took for granted the luxury I lived in. One morning father asked me to deliver a package to a house just a few doors down our street. I stamped my foot and refused, saying, 'I will not be seen carrying a parcel!' Father replied, 'One day, my girl, you may have to travel third class.'

Already I had a very snobbish attitude to life. It had to be all about me. I worshipped my father though, adored him, and always knew I was his favourite. Whenever I wanted something I could easily schmooze him by climbing up on his lap and sniffling his balding head like a little puppy dog. He smelt so good. His aftershave is still so much a part of my memory. One sniffle and he gave into whatever I wanted.

One afternoon as the maid brought the tea things through to us in the living room, father was telling us a joke. He was always jokey, always fun and always having us in stitches. This one was hilarious and tears poured down mother's face.

'Quick, quick, Nicky,' she cried, 'fetch me a bucket, I am going to wet myself!'

As she said this she fell back on the sofa. She didn't move. She was dead. A stroke, the doctor said. Every minute of every hour through the long night that followed I could hear father roaring, 'Come back, come back!' as he sat with mother's body. Between his convulsive sobs he moaned and howled like a wounded animal. His pain invaded every corner of the apartment and of my heart. I didn't know how to comfort him. After mother's body was taken away Hilde and I tiptoed and whispered in the silence that was left behind. All the curtains were drawn and everywhere was dark. Occasionally we heard

5

father's uncontrollable sobs. Days passed in shadows and tears. I cried for my father. At eight-years-old, death was not really a reality but my father's pain was. A few days later he came to me and knelt down, putting his arms around me, hugging me close. When I looked into his eyes one eye was filled with blood from a burst blood vessel. I felt scared at what was happening to him.

'Everything has changed,' he said, 'we will not pray again in this house. There is no God,' he spoke gently. I needed to make things better for him so I said, 'When I grow up will you marry me?' He hugged me tight, 'Yes, my darling, I promise.'

Two years later, only two years later, father announced he was getting married and introduced us to a woman he called our new mother-to-be. I was beside myself with fury. My anger burned inside me, a volcanic eruption waiting to explode. I became rebellious, answering back, sulking. If this new 'mother-to-be' came into the room, I walked out. I left an atmosphere like a bad smell wherever I went. My bad behaviour didn't get rid of her. I had to take a final step to show her how much I did not want this woman to marry my father. He was mine.

Of course, now I am ashamed of my behaviour. But then I would have done anything to keep father to myself. I confronted him and told him I would run away if he married this woman. It was her or me. It worked and he broke it off. I had won. I stopped my sulky moods and all was good again. Two years later father met Martha and this time he was not going to buckle under my demands.

Why had I behaved so badly back then? The first woman I rejected was an angel compared to Martha. After the wedding she demanded we all call her mother. Oh how I hated her and she knew it. I made hell for her and she made hell for me.

When we went away on holiday she would make me sit alone at another table in the dining room. She made me feel like an outsider, rejected. Later on when I became an adult we got on much better but it took a long time.

Father had a great ambition for me to become a concert pianist. Lessons, lessons, lessons ... practice, practice, practice. My life was filled with music but it was not my burning ambition. I loved it and still do. Music is so important but not quite important enough. What I really wanted to do was to dance. My body ached to dance. After my final exam I broke the news to father. He was bitterly disappointed. Of course, he still let me go to the Academy. With his blessing I enrolled at the Mary Wigman Academy of Dance.

Excited yet feeling shy I rang the doorbell. The first day of my new life was about to begin. A gawky young man answered the door. He later told me that he had fallen in love with me on first sight. He was of no interest to me. When he smiled he showed his gums, how repulsive. No, not for me. He was exceptionally persistent in his pursuit of me. I was enjoying the chase. I took my time before falling in love with him. Besides, I was having such a good time. Life was full of fun. I was being introduced to history of art, poetry, literature and through it all, I flirted.

Home had not been fun for so long. I was in love with what I was doing and my new bohemian friends; in love with dance and expressing myself. I have never liked classical ballet. This modern ballet allowed me to express emotion, to feel free. I loved being adored. I needed to feel loved. I couldn't get enough. Ernest, the gawky young man who had opened the door to me on my first day, overpowered me with the force of his love. Soon we planned to marry.

Father was furious, 'You're too young,' he argued, 'he is

only after your money. What future can a dancer give you? You have always lived in luxury. Do you think you can survive poverty? I forbid this marriage. If you go through with it I will disinherit you.'

I was so angry with him. Years of anger, frustration, and pain were all I could feel. How dare father promise to marry me when he knew he couldn't? How dare he tell me I can't marry Ernest? How dare he be disappointed with me for giving up the piano? I'll show him.

I persuaded Ernest to run away with me. Not for long, just long enough for father to become sick with worry. I knew this would really hurt him. He deserved it.

Father was beside himself when he found the note I left him. He phoned the police and reported me missing. He got the radio station to put out a message begging me to come home. Of course, when I heard that we came back immediately. Father looked shattered, like a broken man, and he cried when we walked in. I have had to live with how often I hurt my father. I wanted to punish him and hurt him. I loved him so much, how could I? I will always be haunted by my bad behaviour. The future denied me a chance to make it up to him and to show him how much I loved him.

Ernest and I married on April 13th, 1933 with my father's blessing. By 1934 I was an established dancer with a star-studded career ahead of me. In July 1934 I gave birth to my daughter, Esther, and three weeks later I was a solo dancer in the Salzburg Festival. I was tasting fame and loving it. Soon the air of persecution was seeping into our daily lives. Jews were forbidden to sit in cafés. 'Jew' became a dirty word. Fear was like a silent fog that chilled the air. Ernest and I were due to give a recital. About two hours before the performance we had a call. It was the Gestapo. They warned me that if I went on stage they would arrest me. Ernest could perform, as he was not Jewish. Leaflets were distributed that said, 'If you are a good Nazi you will not attend this performance.' I felt rage tear through my body. No one tells me what I can or cannot do. My stubborn streak ruled me. I had a British passport, thanks to Ernest, and they couldn't touch me. My friends tried to talk sense to me

'The Nazis can do what they like. Be sensible. Think of your baby, don't risk your life,' they pleaded. They were right and I did see sense. The theatre was quite full but hushed. SS men stood in strategic positions along the side of the auditorium. With my heart thumping I stood hidden backstage in the wings. The director announced that I would not be performing and Ernest would dance as though I was. He gestured for me to come forward. I walked onto the stage and someone appeared and presented me with a large bouquet of flowers. I retreated clutching my flowers, giving a bow back into the wings as Ernest danced. You could almost see me with him as he gestured to where I would have been had I been dancing. At the end the audience broke into thunderous applause and cried out, 'Dance Lotte, dance!' I felt triumphant and came forward. More flowers were thrown at my feet. As the applause died down I shouted out to them, 'Thank you for not being Nazis!' Immediately the waiting SS rushed onto the stage screaming, 'Out, out!'

The next morning my money and passport were confiscated. They had to return them though. Without that passport I would not be here today and Esther would not have had a life.

Hitler changed my life and Ernest saved it. Ernest was born in Germany, as was his father. He inherited an English passport from his grandfather, who I presume was born in England and ended up in Germany somehow. Passing on British nationality at that time ended after two generations which meant that Esther has no right to an English passport. I did not know that at the time and applied for her to have her own passport. Probably the clerk who dealt with her application didn't understand either, or maybe it was his first day on the job because without hesitation he gave her a British passport, saving her life.

I did not fancy moving to England. To me it seemed a country with little culture. The women were pear-shaped and the men played cricket. How could I fit into that kind of society? No, I wanted to go to Israel. Again friends put me straight, 'You have to go to England. It would be foolish not to as you are now British.'

It made sense and now I started trips back and forth to England. Sometimes I would go on my own, others with Ernest, leaving Esther with Mimi. Each trip we explored the possibilities of work, of where to live. We also smuggled money out of Germany. That was terrifyingly dangerous. If we had been caught it would have meant an immediate death sentence. Our suitcases not only held a few clothes but also sheet music and manuscripts. In between each page a few notes of paper money were hidden. I also split my sanitary towels and stuffed what I was able to into them.

On one of theses smuggling trips I had a bad feeling. The train sat in the station with its engine throbbing and my heart felt the same way. I waited, dreading to hear the sound of the Gestapo marching the length of the platform seeing who they could haul out. My carriage was full. Fear and silence paralysed us all. I looked up at my suitcase on the rack with the others and wondered if my end had come. Suddenly the sound of the train's engine changed from a throb to a higher pitch. It jerked slowly as though it could hardly pull its weight and moved forward. We all smiled at each other, we had made it! As the train pulled into the border station at Achen it stopped. The heavy footfall of German soldiers marched along the platform. We could hear the sound of train doors being pulled open and the shouting of soldiers cracked the air.

'You, you, you, out!' demanded a soldier pointing at two elderly women in my carriage, and me. We were marched up the platform and I was taken to a shed-like building where a rather large woman with heavy breasts and a sullen face ordered me to undress. I refused, arguing she had no right as I had a British passport. She wasn't impressed, making it clear that I had no choice. Thankfully she let me keep my under-wear on; satisfied I wasn't hiding anything concealed in my clothes. I was ordered to dress and go. I had most of my clothes back on when I realized the train was starting its engine to move off. No way was it going to wait for the poor people running down the platform. I was young and nimble and ran for my life, jumping on the train as it began to move. My blouse flapped open as I clutched it to keep it on. Gasping for breath I felt elated that I had made it. I looked up to see my suitcases still on the rack. The other two empty seats in our carriage stayed empty.

In 1938 I left for England for good. Esther and I were free and safe. We had a room in a house filled with refugees. The atmosphere felt relaxed, and everyone was in the same boat. There were three floors of chattering, laughing people, some practising on instruments they managed to bring over. Each floor had a gas stove on the landing that all the families had to share.

Ernest wrote me a letter letting me know when he would be arriving and saying, 'You will have to eat a lot of bread when I get to you.' It turned out that one of his suitcases was filled with bread rolls. He had removed their insides and stuffed them with money.

I couldn't live without Mimi so we arranged for her to come and live with us. I hated housework and Mimi had been with us since the day Esther was born. She was employed to look after Esther but once she was with us in England she ended up looking after all of us. Mimi was glad to get out of Germany. Although she was not Jewish she hated what was happening and no doubt, as a sympathizer, would have soon ended up in a camp. We only had one bed and this we bartered with Mimi. She gave us her sugar ration and we slept on the floor; a perfect solution. Ernest and I always had a sweet tooth, which we paid for later.

I got a job as a model in Chelsea Art School and hated it. I went to Madame Rambert and got some occasional work with her. Modern ballet wasn't popular with the British who preferred their ballet classical. This made finding work a struggle. It was the commercial world that offered the most work. As well as some teaching, I later toured with E.N.S.A. [Entertainments National Service Association].

To start with I think that Ernest was having some kind of breakdown. Every day he would just play Patience or some other card game with friends. 'Get out, get a job!' I shouted at him in despair.

We managed to find and move into a cheap little flat and I started an affair. I was still shouting at Ernest to get a job. At last he must have heard me. For three nights running Ernest took his violin and played on Kilburn Bridge, his beret at his feet. He came home with his beret filled with pennies and sixpenny pieces. 'How could you?' I yelled at him, 'How could you? I am so ashamed of you, what a dreadful thing to do. I am so angry ... you're a criminal!' I took the three shillings he had made and said to my lover, 'Come on, let's go to the cinema. Ernest's begging money can pay.' I so wanted to hurt Ernest for what he had done.

In 1939 father and Martha fled to Holland. In 1941 they were caught with many other Jews and marched into the cattle trucks. They were taken to Auschwitz. In 1943 I was given the news that father had been taken to the gas chamber to die with that day's quota. I remember running down the street howling, shouting, screaming. A woman from an upstairs window leant out and called, 'What's wrong, love?'

I sobbed through gasps, 'My father's been killed in the gas chamber.'

'Come on up here, love, let me make you a cup of tea', she called down. I did. The kindness of that stranger meant so much to me at that moment."

Two

1939, England. My last chat with Opa.

If only I could have been born a grown-up and escaped all that childhood angst.

One of my mother's students, a regular for many years at her famous studio, said to mother's assistant, Lois, 'Lotte is fabulous, isn't she? What a character, so charismatic, so dynamic, so scary ... but I wouldn't want her for my mother!'

I laughed when I heard that. She was right. Mother wasn't the easiest person to have as a parent but if I had to choose it would be her every time. With her, life was never black and white, never predictable, never stable. It was a mixture of great fun and great pain, with a very different kind of morality. No, I wouldn't change a thing. I have benefited from having her as my mother. Both my sons have benefited from having her as their grandmother. It made life very colourful. Her philosophy has influenced us all:

be honest
be selfish
be yourself.

★

Mother always called herself a *refujew*, complaining that she did not belong to any country.

"I will never be English," she would say.

She hated if anyone thought she was from Germany, though. She liked people to think she was French – such a sexy accent.

It took me nearly a lifetime to truly appreciate my parents for who they were. I tried not to let them know my feelings and only later in life did I feel able to show my love, despite frequent rejection. It took me a long time to learn to value my parents instead of seeing them through the eyes of a child that felt unloved and abandoned. As a girl, my desire to always try to please got me into trouble. I was told not to smile; mother found the sight of my gums ugly. Somehow I never got it right. Frequently mother would press her finger on the tip of my nose, pushing it up.

"I don't want you to develop a Jewish nose," she would say as she scrutinized my face. "A snub nose would be much more attractive."

I developed an introverted and withdrawn personality and even as an adult I have great difficulty in standing up for myself with people and situations new to me.

There was only one occasion when I really let my mother know how I was feeling as a child. I was about 11 or 12 verging on adolescence. We were staying at my Aunty Margaret's house in Winchelsea, Sussex. She was my father's sister, a woman full of fun and laughter. She drank and smoked with great gusto, more than most men. The house rocked when she played boogie-woogie on the piano, ash flying everywhere.

Mother was always falling in love and attracting admirers. Even Aunty Margaret had a crush on her, but mother was sleeping with Uncle Bob, Aunty Margaret's husband, at the time. Throughout all her romantic tumult, I was the ear that mother used most to recount unwelcome, explicit details of the sexual side of her love life. At 12 I was too young to handle those intimate details and I remember feeling very uncomfortable.

At this time, my father's brother, Frank, and his wife and six children were also visiting Aunty Margaret. Their lives looked a lot more fun than my lonely life in London. With six new brothers and sisters I thought I might never be lonely again and I wouldn't have to listen to all the gory details about my mother's sex life either.

"I want to be adopted. I don't want to live with a prostitute," I said, boldly.

As the words came out of my mouth I saw the look on her face and knew that I had gone too far. I had never experienced stunned silence from my mother before. She always liked to have the last word. I was consumed with terror as I saw her black eyes grow large and it felt as if they were drilling holes into every part of my body.

Mother's answer shot out of her mouth like a bullet, 'NO!'

She turned and left the room. No chat. No questions. Just the empty room and the realisation that perhaps the word 'prostitute' wasn't very nice or was it 'adoption'? I'll never know.

★

"One day when you've grown up you will be as beautiful as your mother," a family friend once reassuringly told me, believing that maybe I felt ugly because I had such a beautiful mother. I hadn't really noticed that I was probably a gawky, unattractive child. What I did feel was lonely and isolated. I didn't seem to belong to the world but stood on the edge looking in and dreaming of ways of joining in. Mimi, who had cared for me since the day I was born, was the one constant and reliable person in my life, but she left to work for another family when I was about six. Her love and warmth had given me important security in my early years. Despite her leaving, we stayed good friends throughout her life. There was such a special bond between us. She came to my wedding. When my first baby, Michael, was born Mimi was the person I most wanted to show him off to.

After Mimi left, mother and father had a succession of young girls living in to look after me. What with my parents' work and touring, mother moving in with a new lover or a new lover moving in, I was left in a limbo of disconnected threads of life. I didn't understand the world and I couldn't make sense of life. I felt disoriented during those childhood years. I became quite passive. Mother showed quite aggressive behaviour. Her dominating personality made her someone I was more afraid of than comfortable with.

As a girl I would frequently find myself alone in the flat, especially during school holidays. I would get a hug, a kiss, and a, 'Goodbye, be good,' from my parents and then the front door would click shut and I was on my own, free to do what I enjoyed most. I would put on a record I loved to dance to. *Rhapsody in Blue* was a favourite. We had a good collection of classical records, which my parents would sit and listen to as if they were at an actual concert. I found listening to them in that grown up way far too boring. Instead of that, I would find a stool to stand on. Then, using a blackboard pointer as a baton, I would be transformed into a conductor. I had always been fascinated by the conductors when I was taken to concerts. They made such dramatic movements, their heads thrusting this way and that, their body alive to the thrill of their power and of the music. I wanted to feel that. Unfortunately, my musical education only went as far as learning three time and four time. I never noticed the difference. Bach, Beethoven and Mozart all got the same treatment, whatever the piece. Luckily they were dead and my parents were out, so I got away with it.

I spent most of my childhood in this way and could occupy myself for hours. When I got bored with conducting or dancing I went to the cinema. This being the 1940s, children had to be accompanied by an adult. So, to get in, I would try to make myself look older by putting on a headscarf and pair of mother's high heels (size sevens). Thus dressed I would totter precariously to the Shepherd's Bush Empire. There was always a queue for the cinema in those days. I would walk along the queue asking each adult in turn, 'Please, would you take me in with you? I have money for the ticket.' Most of the time a kind soul would take pity and allow me to walk in with them. Once inside the comfort of the darkness I would go off and sit on my own. Sometimes I would sit right through to the second showing. I might as well get my money's worth, hey? It never mattered how many times I saw a film, it was always magic being drawn into that other world. I can see there were reasons why I had such a love of this other world and was so happy entertaining myself. The life of the child is so often one of powerlessness and one of being at the mercy of others. What a blessing to have the possibility of escape through the imagination.

I was eight-years-old when my parents answered an ad in the paper. It had been put there by a family looking for a little girl to board with them and be company for their daughter who was about two years older than me. They lived in a nice, conventional flat in Chiswick, a short walk from the school I was going to attend. In retrospect I can only imagine that the parents of this girl must have put the advert out because of the difficulties they were having with her. Now these difficulties became mine, too.

It began with her pushing me down some concrete steps, ordering me to climb back up and then pushing me down them again and again. The block of flats had back stairs and there she would have me stand on the top step until she pushed me from behind. Down I would fall only to have to climb back up again. I can still see the grey, cold concrete of those steps. It was a ritual: push, down I'd go, up I would climb, push ... She frequently beat me with a blackboard stick. My body became bruised and weals came up on my back. I must have been a total joy for her because my consuming fear of her every move kept me compliant to her every wish. I do not know if her family was Christian but I do remember the size of the bible this girl used to hit me. As I sat on my bed, bang, down it would come, large and heavy, the leather binding hard against my head. She told me this was the sort of treatment I could expect when I went to boarding school and she was helping me get used to it. Was this true? I had been told I would be going to boarding school when I turned nine years old. Was this really what I could expect there?

One bath night her mother came to wash me down and was horrified at the sight of my body. I was covered in bruises. She asked me what had happened. I was so terrified of what punishment her daughter would have in store for me if I told the truth that I said that I'd fallen down the stairs. No more was said.

Apart from these flashes of memory I do not remember much about what happened at this time. Perhaps it is a blessing that I have almost a total blank. This girl and I went to the same school and had to walk there together. There was no escaping her. I went home every weekend and would beg my mother to take me away, to not make me go back to that family, but she refused. I grew more and more frightened of returning and dreaded Monday mornings when I was put on the bus to go back.

One weekday afternoon mother came to Chiswick to visit me, which was most unusual. We all sat in the smart sitting room and drank tea from bone china cups. I remember mother was wearing brown corduroy trousers; as we sat there, my fingers traced along the ridges of them. I could only look down. I'd whisper to my mother, 'Please, please take me home.' Again, she wouldn't relent.

Each day became more of a nightmare until I could bear it no more. After a weekend at home, once again I was put on the bus for Chiswick – this time on a Sunday evening instead of the usual Monday morning. I was given my three-penny piece and told to be a good girl. As the bus slowed down at my stop I instinctively ducked down to avoid being seen by the person who would be waiting to collect me. As the bus drove on I felt overwhelming joy. I was free! Not that I knew what to do next. Unsure, I got off at the next stop, crossed the road and waited for a bus to take me back home to Shepherd's Bush. When I told the bus conductor I'd lost my fare he couldn't have been nicer. That was the first time anyone called me 'luv'. As I walked in to our block of flats my Aunt Hilde and her husband were walking out. They lived on the fifth floor of the same block as my parents. I explained that I had run away. They were on their way out for dinner and said that I had better join them as my parents were out. It was the first 'posh' restaurant that I had been to and I had a fairytale evening. I remember the sensation as I fingered the crisp linen tablecloth. Everyone was so nice and I felt like a princess. Sadly, it didn't last. When mother returned she was angry and adamant that I could not stay at home. I was sent back the next morning and was to remain there until the end of term.

Some years later my mother confessed to me the reason why I had been sent away. She had fallen in love with an Indian academic and poet called Vallathol K Narayana Menon who had recently published a book on Yeats and lived on the 7th floor of our block. As we lived on the 10th floor there was quite a bit of to and fro which had been hampered by my presence. Sending me away made things less complicated for them, freeing them to have more time with each other. This man had meant so much to my mother that when he moved back home to India she nearly went with him. However, she got cold feet and decided to stay in England. When she later discovered she was pregnant by him she aborted the baby.

I did go to boarding school. It was Burgess Hill in Surrey, one of the early experimental, progressive schools and one that was probably more liberal than the famous Summerhill. This was another bewildering experience for me. I was too shy to mix with the other children. As there were no rules about having to go into lessons, I decided not to. I was too afraid of showing my ignorance, too afraid of rejection. I spent many hours alone playing in the sand pit.

Although at times my childhood was lonely and painful, there were good things about having such unconventional parents. They were dancers, which to me was such an exciting life, a life that I could be a little part of by seeing them up there on stage, watching rehearsals, going backstage during performances, meeting glamorous chorus girls who giggled and threw their arms about as they chatted. The dancers called me darling and often cuddled and kissed me. I loved it all: the colourful make-up, the big, black eyes, the eye lashes so long that they tickled their eyebrows, the lipstick so red it made a splash and a gash. Oh, it was wonderful. There was music and laughter, shouting and chaos. Perhaps this was the real world. I just loved it. These times of joy were rare and precious. They lit up my world. I wanted more than anything to be part of that happy and colourful life.

Three

A holiday in Ireland.

At 13-years-old I went to drama school. I felt that going on stage at least had some fun and glamour to it. Sadly, a lack of understanding of how to learn drove me to dislike regular lessons and school in general. At 15 I left school for good, thinking, 'At last I'm a grown-up.' My parents were performing in Bournemouth at this time and they found me a job in a summer show as a comedian's feed. It was a laugh and I had a great time. Most of all I was just so glad that I was no longer a child.

Next came panto season and I was a Red Indian brave in Peter Pan. But what to do after that? Mother scoured *The Stage* and found an ad calling for showgirls for a nightclub in Paris. I have no doubt the fact that Paris was her favourite city influenced her as she pushed me to audition. The fact I would perform nude or near nude didn't trouble her at all, but it bothered me.

Nudity, in fact, was a big part of my family life. My father was what is now called a naturist and insisted that mother and I take our clothes off at home. I did this until I was about 13-years-old. He thought that it was natural and healthy to not wear clothes. I was never at ease with this, feeling exposed and as if I was being looked at with dirty eyes. My father was definitely lecherous, especially to young girls – even me. Despite my shame I felt powerless to object. Mother was not comfortable with it either and insisted that she kept her bra and pants on. She didn't like to see my father naked and would complain, 'I don't want to see your dangly bits while I'm eating my breakfast.'

The audition was held by a charming Frenchman named Rene Bardy. He was short and round and similar to Poirot, sort of cuddly and fatherly with a delightful smile. However, when he asked me to remove my sweater and then my bra I was overtaken with embarrassment. I got the job, though. It was a in a club called Chez Eve at Place Pigalle.

I sometimes wonder whether mother should ever have had a child. She was not maternally inclined. Having had seven abortions herself during those dark days before abortion was legalised, it was natural for her to set me up with proper contraception before I left for Paris. She took me to the Marie Stopes Clinic to be fitted with a 'Dutch cap'. At that time the clinic would only do this for married women so mother dressed me up in her clothes and make-up and transformed me from a girl of 16 years to a young woman at least five years older.

I staggered to the Tube in high heels, clinging to my mother. When we arrived at the clinic and sat in the waiting room she took off her wedding ring and slipped it on my finger.

"There, that's looking more convincing," she said as she smiled and squeezed my hand.

When I was admitted, the consulting room was large and empty and the one examination couch seemed to disappear in the starkness of everything around it.

"You see, my dear, you squeeze the cap just so and slip it up at this angle and in just a second it's all in place, nothing to it."

The nurse demonstrated, and yes, up it slipped. It didn't seem to be too difficult.

"I'm going to leave you to it now. Just relax and practise, you'll get the hang of it in no time. Back soon."

Her shoes echoed on the worn linoleum floor and the door closed behind her. I was alone. With my knees bent up, and feeling very exposed, I started to push the contraption up. I wasn't used to touching myself and was, quite frankly, ignorant about what was between my legs. After several attempts I became a bit sore but, suddenly, I did it. Before I could enjoy my success, I noticed with horror I was no longer wearing my mother's ring. Panic set in. I was so ignorant that I wasn't sure what would have happened to those things inside me. How far had they gone? Was it like eating? Would they have disappeared? Well, there was nothing else to do but to put my hand back up inside and delve about while at the same time trying to discover the trick of removing the cap. It was unknown territory. I became an explorer in a foreign land. Quick, quick, the nurse would be returning any second. I fumbled frantically and, then, a miracle. First I felt the ring and then I managed to get the cap out just as the door opened and the nurse returned with a comforting smile.

"There, that wasn't so bad, was it?"

I had already lost my virginity. (Why do we use that expression, *lost*? It's almost as if it could be recovered, perhaps by advertising: 'Lost, virginity, reward if found.') I lost mine in Bournemouth. I was 15-years-old. I didn't mean to lose it. It was taken with no please or thank you by the producer of the show my parents worked in, in our family hotel suite while my parents were out. He was a big, heavy man. I didn't know what to do. I was a flirtatious young girl but I never thought it would lead to this. I fought him off, pushing hard against his stomach, my thumbs and fist digging into his flabby flesh. I was a slip of a girl and didn't stand a chance.

When my parents returned I told them what had happened, that I had been raped.

"Look," they said. "Let's agree to forget about it. We could all lose our jobs."

It was never mentioned again.

★

Paris. I truly grew up in Paris. Everything about it excited me. I revelled in how different everything was from anything else I had known. The city felt vibrant and alive.

I even grew to love working at Chez Eve. Once I got over the self-conscious embarrassment of wearing very little on stage, I enjoyed every second. Luckily I have two beautiful big scars on my stomach from a peritonitis operation so I was allowed to wear a little something on my lower half. The club was small, intimate and discreet with soft lighting. Small, circular tables surrounded the glass stage and we were lit up from underneath. We worked until three a.m. and then fell into the restaurant next door for a late supper of steak and fries with a rum and coke, or perhaps made our way to a bistro close by for a very early breakfast of eggs and bacon with lots of French bread washed down with hot milk and rum. This was the height of decadence for me; I was drinking alcohol for the first time and always eating out.

My solo number was my greatest delight. Thanks to my scars my costume was a small tambourine that sat round my hips. It was supposed to look as though I had stepped into it.

It jingled when I walked and wiggled my hips. I held an umbrella which had beads sewn all over it that hung down at different lengths like rain drops. I twisted and twirled wearing nothing else but a wicked grin as I danced to *Lady Be Good*. If I was doing it now I would do *Raindrops Keep Falling on my Head*.

During the day I'd go out exploring Paris with my favourite girlfriend, Red. I never did find out how she came to be called that. Together we burnt the candle right through but never felt tired. Walking through the streets of Paris arm-in-arm with Red, I was overcome by the strangeness of a new city. It was so different to London. Red and I explored all her streets, laughing at I can't remember what and always broke. As we wandered along one day, taking it all in, we saw a cinema advertising the film, *An American in Paris*.

"We'll have to see that," I elbowed Red.

A few days later, we did. We both stifled our laughter at hearing a French-speaking Gene Kelly.

Shopping in Paris in the 1950s was a dream compared to England. Everything looked so fashionable. I blew a week's wages on a pencil skirt – the first and most fashionable item I'd ever bought. I felt I looked as though I'd just stepped out of *Vogue*. Next week's wages went on my first high heels. No matter how much my feet hurt as we walked street after street with Red pulling me along, I kept them on. She could totter over cobbles and still look great. My blisters bled but I wouldn't give in and continued to bear the pain so long as I thought that I looked a million dollars.

What was it about Paris that made me love her so? When it rained, she glistened and shone. When windy she blew the streets clean. When the sun shone, a lazy stroll down by the Seine filled my heart with such happiness. It was a beautiful, new feeling. I felt fresh and free. I was right, being grown up was a lot better than being a child. At 16 I did not know about all the serious growing up I had yet to do.

Red and I started going regularly to the Left Bank, where she knew an artist. He introduced us to some American art students, one of which, Jay, developed a crush on me. I started to learn about the thrills of young romance. Every experience was new and raw and I felt that nothing would ever be as exciting again. Although unbeknownst to me another adventure was just about to unfold.

My life in Paris ended rather abruptly. I had no work permit and was under-age, which neither my mother nor I had realised. A jealous dancer at the club reported me for breaking the law. We were reported to the Home Office and I had to leave pronto. Back in England there was a court case where I faced a barrage of questions designed to catch me out into confessing that I had known I was working illegally. Thankfully, my genuine innocence came through. Mother could have been given a six-month prison sentence but fortunately she escaped with a £2 fine and we were free to go.

All through the ordeal I was bombarded with the most wonderful cards from Jay, each with a hilarious hand-drawn cartoon. How I pined to go back to Paris but I couldn't see how it was possible with no job and nowhere to stay. So, instead, I embarked on another exhilarating love affair. I still felt the pull to return to Paris but this romance, with the famous art critic David Sylvester, was my first serious sexual relationship and temporarily took my mind off any thoughts of returning to France. David was such an exciting person to be around. He was a close friend of Francis Bacon, publishing several books on his work, and conducting the most interesting interviews with him. I hadn't at first realised that I wasn't

David's number one girlfriend, or that there were even any other girlfriends. When I found out I challenged him to choose. He didn't choose me. I was so peeved and self righteous and strong about this – how dare he? – that I moved quickly on to the next adventure. Through David, however, I started to realise that it was the art as much as the man that was stimulating me. So began my love affair with the art world, an affair that would soon continue in Paris.

★

'Go and sit in the Dome. Just sit there and wait. You won't be waiting for long, I promise the guys will take good care of you,' Jay wrote. In his letter, accompanied by his amusing cartoons of mice in berets sitting in bars, strolling down streets and sipping aperitifs, he told me he was off to Amsterdam on an art scholarship for three months and offered me the use of his room in Paris while he was away. It was too good an offer to refuse. I quickly took the train back to France and installed myself in his attic room in Hotel des Bains in rue Delambre.

Jay was right. He had left instructions for all his friends to take good care of me and they certainly did. My first day back in Paris as I sat in the Dome, sipping a coca cola, an American voice drawled in my ear, 'Hi, you must be Jay's friend.'

Soon another young man came by, and another. 'This is terrific,' I thought to myself. I was so scared of being lonely and of not having Jay's shoulder to lean on and his bed to share. Thanks to him, I had become a little honey pot and I liked all the bees I was attracting. I was at the centre of quite a group of students from the American Art College. We all became firm friends. They liked this little English girl and wanted to look after me. I felt happy and secure and suddenly didn't miss

Jay at all. The days seemed to pass with very little purpose. There didn't seem to be much evidence of attending college. We drifted about. They took me with them as they visited each other's studios and then spent long hours in The Dome in Montparnasse, or across the street in Le Select, discussing art, philosophy and sex. It was more than I could have wished for.

Despite discussions of the higher things in life, flirting was the name of the game in Parisian cafes. And so it was one day at The Dome when I noticed a handsome man with olive skin and beautiful eyes looking at me with deep intensity. As he sipped his cola he hardly broke his gaze. The cafe was quiet that day and there was no question that it was me on the receiving end of those long, lingering looks. Unusually, I wasn't with my group of friends that day. My mother was paying me a visit and I was showing her some of my haunts. I leaned over to her.

"Don't look, but that gorgeous man at the table to your left keeps staring at me."

Many times I have been asked what Yves Klein's first words to me were but I can only remember the feeling of paralysis that spread through my body and into my brain when he first appeared beside our table. It was a strong, chemical reaction, changing the blood in my veins to lukewarm water and my mind to jelly.

Whatever it was he said, somehow a meeting was arranged and we began a gloriously lustful and happy relationship. Yves was a budding painter at that time and lived with his parents in a large, rambling house. They were also painters and every Saturday they held an open house for artists and poets. Painters would bring canvases to show and poets would read their work.

I moved into this world of art and literature, not understanding much, but loving the air of excitement and trying so hard to make sense of it all. At night I would sleep curled in Yves' arms on a mattress on the floor of his room. A chaos of clothes and clutter lay about us and the smell of oil paint penetrated every corner of the room and of the house. It was a fertile place for the nurturing of a young artist.

Paris was, and is, the most invigorating city and each time I have returned to her I have fallen deeper in love. Yet at that time I felt a growing restlessness, an urge to get away. I found myself missing England and needing some time to myself. Yves was increasingly absorbed in his work and living in such a vibrant and busy household as the Kleins' was starting to stretch my nerves and make me feel claustrophobic.

I decided that the time had come for a visit home to my parents. Yves was upset and insisted that we should get engaged before I left. I agreed but he soon had to accept that I was determined to go and the day soon came when he reluctantly took me to the station for what we both thought would be a brief parting. It was, in fact, the end of our life together.

I was pleased when later Yves became famous for his blue paintings. Nine years after I met him he patented his 'International Klein Blue' (IKB). By that time he was history for me. Many years later both my sons were at art college and learned about this great artist. I was so pleased to know they both felt a connection with this man whom I had loved.

As Yves carried my bags into my compartment I noticed from the corner of my eye my travelling companion was a handsome young man. I was conscious of his eyes on me as Yves returned to the platform and I did that romantic thing I had seen in films such as the heartbreaking *Brief Encounter*, theatrically hanging out of the window and deeply kissing my lover goodbye. There must have been a streak of mischief in my blood as I could feel the sizzling and tingling through my body and I was very aware of my audience of one. As the train moved slowly out of the station Yves ran along the platform, still clutching my hand until his legs could go no faster and his hand slipped from mine. We waved and waved, his figure receding as the train gathered speed.

I sat down opposite the young man and we soon exchanged names. By the time we arrived in England, Peter and I had also exchanged phone numbers. Now, although I liked Peter – he had made a boring journey more pleasant and there is nothing like a little light flirting to give you a glow – I had decided I didn't need or want to see him again. When he phoned me a few days later to invite me out I was about to say no when he told me we would be going to a party hosted by Dylan Thomas. Of course the opportunity to meet a poet I so admired was too good to miss and I agreed to go, vowing to myself that I would not go out with Peter again after this. And I didn't. This was not, however, because Yves was waiting for me in Paris, but because it was at this party I was swept off my feet by the man I was to marry.

★

Last year, after a 54-year break, I went back to Paris. This time I went with my grown up sons, Jo and Michael. As we sat in Le Select drinking freshly pressed orange juice they tried to imagine their mother's life, to see Paris through my eyes. Little had changed. The cafes were still there, the hotels. The only things missing were my youth and the beautiful young men that made Paris what it was for me.

Four

John & I enjoying the garden.

Dylan Thomas' party was in full swing. It was May 24, 1952. As I walked into his house, a throbbing beat of music filled the air. There were people sprawled on sofas, standing up against doors and coupling in darkened corners.

"Haven't you got a drink?" someone said as they jostled into me.

The room was full and people spilled out through the French doors into the night.

"You can sleep in my wet bed any night," another drunk said as he lurched towards me.

I decided to skip the drink and the invitation. As I made my way out to the garden I could still feel the warmth of the day in the balmy evening air. A man was climbing a dead tree stump. He was clutching his stomach.

"I am in agony. I am only climbing this tree to stop the pain," he called to me.

I didn't think anything of it, bizarre as the scene was. My mother often had severe stomach pain. Hers was due to chronic constipation. John's, as we later found out, was an ulcer. He came down from the tree, putting his arms around me and started to dance, singing:

"I'm going to take you away to Spain."

Suddenly, he let go and held his stomach, the pain getting between us. We were joined by another man, who placed his arms around me and led me in a dance. He and I moved well together. We chatted. We weren't as drunk as most of Dylan's guests. Later, when we were introduced, I learned that he was the poet David Wright. I was surprised at how easily we had chatted as he was totally deaf. His skill at lip reading amazed me.

What a party. The drunks got drunker. The noise got louder. A voice shouted down. I looked where it had come from. At the top of the stairs stood Dylan's wife, Caitlin. With anger in her voice she shouted:

"You can all get out! Go on! Get out, now!"

She sounded as though this wasn't the first time she had had to throw people out. Dylan wasn't about any more. Maybe he had had enough himself and gone to bed. Everyone seemed to have had more than enough. John searched me out and grabbed my arm:

"Come on, I'm going to get a taxi and see you home."

I was impressed; a staggering, rolling drunk who could still be a gentleman. A group of us squeezed into the taxi and as we trundled along someone said, "Bloomsbury." Everyone got out, the taxi was paid for and it drove off. It appears that we had only got in to bum a ride. John and I walked and walked through the empty streets. An occasional taxi passed by, but not for us. John had no money on him at all and I had only two shillings. As John walked me towards Kensington and home, to my surprise he stopped and turned to me, pointing:

"Well, I go down this road to get to mine. You just follow that one to get to Shepherd's Bush."

After making arrangements to see each other the next day,

off he went, singing tunelessly, weaving along the pavement. Still left with a long, solitary walk home, I hailed the next taxi and asked how far two shillings would take me.

"How far do you want to go?" the driver replied with a wry smile.

"Shepherd's Bush."

"Okay, hop in."

Bliss. I relaxed back in the seat. Soon I would be in my bed.

★

"You won't believe it!" I hugged mother. "I've met the man I am going to marry. He is gorgeous. More than gorgeous. More like a film star, a bit of Cary Grant and a Greek god."

And John was. Oh how he took my breath away. He had a touch of the rough and the suave, both sexy and smooth with a James Dean walk. He'd place two cigarettes between his lips, flip open his Zippo and, lighting them, pass one to me. Didn't Humphrey Bogart do that for Ingrid Bergman? I just wanted to tear his clothes off each time we met and after Dylan's party we met every day. For me it was the first time I'd ever experienced real lust. My sexual appetite could not be quenched. John felt the same. A hot, burning love devoured us. I would have walked over hot coals, walked the Arctic for him. Perhaps in my own way, I did.

We spent every evening drinking in the Q.E. (Queen's Elm) in Kensington, a watering hole for painters and writers. I still didn't understand about alcohol and tended not to drink. My parents only drank at parties. I had never seen them drunk. John was drunk every night and in very good company of drunks. John was just as loveable when drunk: loving, affectionate, very good-natured, a happy-go-lucky boy. Sober, he was more of an 'angry young man' with a simmering anger that you could feel.

After a couple of weeks of us dating, I met John's family. At first I fell for his mother. She was Irish, very attractive, knew how to dress with flair, and was incredibly nice. I noticed John kept his distance from her, as well as his brother. They were all very anti-Semitic and didn't like the idea of a Jew being in the family, especially John's grandmother, who always had a drink on the go. In fact, they each drank rum in the kitchen out of little white railway station cups. When the notorious poet George Barker, John's mother's brother, visited, the grandmother didn't want him to have any rum and would shout, 'Quick, hide your cups!'

Three months after we met, we planned a simple wedding – a month after my 18th birthday, by which time I was already six weeks pregnant. John had no job, lived with his dysfunctional mother. And prospects? What a laugh. I must have done a fantastic job of convincing my mother of my love for John. Father wasn't sure about my relationship, though. I suppose that my being pregnant didn't give them much choice to interfere.

August 1952, a drizzly day, my wedding day, I boarded the 49 bus with my parents and dear Mimi. After the service in the register office we met up with our drunken friends across the road at the Bunch of Grapes. To finish the day off, John and I went to the cinema to see the Marx Brothers' *Duck Soup*. After all, we needed a laugh; getting married is a serious business.

★

Although life for my family in England had been a financial struggle, I had never felt poor. I had been provided with a private education. This was because my father had worked as a dance teacher at my school, so although no money changed hands; it was a private education, nonetheless. We lived in a comfortable, centrally heated flat in Shepherd's Bush. It was not grand and it never had a cosy, warm feel but it was quite large. There was even room for my mother's sister Hilde to come and live with us (although whenever my mother moved her current boyfriend in, father was temporarily thrown out). But the flat had never truly felt like home to me. When not sent away to boarding school or summer camp I endured hours and days of loneliness there. Despite our poverty I had never felt financially deprived, only deprived of affection.

When John walked into my life I was yearning for love. As a poet he offered me a liferaft of dreams to float away on. As a young wife and mother I found myself living in total poverty and expected to look after a home and a family. John felt deeply that as a poet he must not prostitute his art by working. Only occasionally, and then driven by hunger, did he take a temporary job: a porter at Paddington Station, a postman over Christmas, a coal man.

I tried to help out, in my way. Obviously working seminude as a dancer was now out of the question. I sewed lampshades at home and became a cleaner for half the rent of our flat – I'd never cleaned anything more than my teeth as a child. I only knew how to cook a couple of dishes: German potato salad, meatloaf and meatballs. That wasn't much help because we couldn't afford meat.

This was not the life John had dreamed of. He was a romantic and we really did try to live off his dreams. They kept us going on cold nights. We'd cuddle together and try to escape our reality through fantasy. A favourite one was of a country cottage and if it could have roses around the door, all the better.

One day John packed his haversack and left to hitchhike around the country and see if he could find our dream cottage. We had just admitted defeat and given up our flat. Baby Michael had arrived and even the low rent we had been paying became impossible to find. My Aunt Margaret came to the rescue, offering us a place to stay over her newsagent's shop in St Albans in exchange for help with the business. So, it was from this shop that two-month old Michael and I waved John on his way. To me, living in St Albans already felt like being in the country but John's dream was for something really remote.

Within days, he returned. A hero, in my eyes, the hunter had slain his quarry and come back with our dream. It was a very small cottage in Dorset. No matter that it was condemned; the landlady, Mrs Rose, had offered it to John rent free if his wife (me) would do some occasional cooking. Knowing my limitations, John had bought me a cookbook and the deal was sealed.

Good old Auntie Margaret sent us off with a few pennies in our pockets and hired us a rickety van with a driver of similar vintage. And so we rattled our way to Dorset. By the time we reached our cottage it was dark and I couldn't make out what it looked like. Although John had gently warned me that the cottage wasn't yet quite what we had dreamed of and that I might find some comforts missing, nothing could have prepared me for the realities of our new home. As we opened the door a strong smell of mould hit me. John had neglected to tell me that we would have no electricity, no lavatory and only one cold tap. We unloaded our few pieces of furniture in the dark. The only potential source of heating was a very old range with an open grate and a tiny oven to one side. Baby Michael had fallen asleep in my arms so I put him down in his cot upstairs while John, holding our only candle, scavenged for sticks in the garden to light a fire in the range. Leaving Michael to sleep, in the pitch darkness I walked downstairs, burst into tears and cried and cried. John left for the pub, a short walk down the road. I felt that I had travelled back in time at least 200 years. I sat shivering from cold and shock.

Yet the worst horror was still to come – the outside lavatory. This was actually a corrugated shed housing a bucket and thousands of insects. Greenery had forced its way in through cracks and was taking over. A plank of wood with a hole in it lay across the bucket. Spiders ran back and forth across this makeshift seat, daring you to sit down. They were some of the largest spiders I had ever seen. As a young child I had once run into a spider's web in the garden and screamed hysterically as I frantically tried to wipe it from my face. This strong fear returned every time I had to use that bucket. No wonder I became chronically constipated for many years to follow.

Gradually, I learnt how to survive in our new home. We had a Tilley lamp that gave out reasonable light in the evenings. I never did master lighting it though so I stuck to candles if John was out. They gave a warm, comforting glow, which would almost have been romantic if the circumstances hadn't been so dire.

I did conquer the Primus stove, with some misgivings. I was afraid each time I primed and pumped it that it would blow up. As it was my chief cooking source, I had little choice but to steel myself and get on with it. I boiled water on this for all our washing, including nappies and also for housework and the occasional cup of tea.

Daily, John and I walked miles collecting wood and piling it up on the pram until only Michael's eyes were visible above the stack. It was hard work but it meant that our evenings would be warm. On the nights that John didn't go to the pub we read stories to each other to help take our minds off our hunger. This didn't happen too often as he had discovered the local cider, which he thought a bargain at sixpence a pint. Somehow he always managed to find a sixpence when he needed a drink. Cigarettes were more of a problem. We tried rolling our own using tealeaves and newspaper. We both held our throats as every drag of this dreadful concoction burnt its way down. John then had a better idea. He would go out walking and, if the weather was dry, pick up dog ends from the road. If it were wet he would look in the telephone boxes for pickings. This only left the problem of finding money for cigarette papers. To help eke things out I was banned from smoking. John said he was unable to work on his poetry without smoking and I believed him. I continued to yearn for nicotine and was pathetically grateful for every occasional puff I was allowed.

My joy at watching Michael grow helped me through the hardship. He was soon pulling himself up, gripping whatever furniture his little hands could hang onto. I became conscious of his tiny, bare feet on the cold stone floor. At 10-months-old he was showing signs of wanting to walk but he had no shoes and we had no proper heating. December that year was particularly cold. Despite his pink cheeks and huge smile, Michael's feet were turning blue. I shuddered at the sight. I had to do something. Perhaps I could wrap them in my woollen gloves? No, he'd pull them off as quickly as I put them on and we'd have a new game. That wouldn't work. It is said that necessity is the mother of invention. So it was. I cut up my leather handbag for soles. Having done that I unravelled one of my woollen sweaters and started knitting. Two squares did the trick. I sewed them up the sides so now I had two small tubes. These I sewed onto the leather soles that I had cut out and, hey presto, Michael had a pair of bootees. I felt thrilled at my achievement.

Knitting had never come naturally to me but now I was left with a sweater with a few rows of wool missing. I thought I might make use of the rest of the wool. I decided to knit Michael a sweater as his were all a bit short and tight, leaving a lot of his soft, pink skin exposed to the weather. I had been taught to cast on and cast off and I could only knit in straight lines, which meant that the sleeves went straight out from the neck. After they were done I cast off a few stitches and continued straight down for the body. I repeated this a second time, sewed up the sides and had a warm, woolly jumper with arms that stuck out straight from the body so it looked like a T-junction sign. Never mind, I thought, and popped him in it. When he put his arms down to the side a large amount of bulk bulged under his arms. That didn't stop me from being proud of my enterprise. I couldn't wait for John to come home and see my achievement: bootees and a sweater in one afternoon!

Mother knew that we were struggling and sometimes sent a postal order for two shillings and sixpence. Otherwise we lived off hope and tick. Despite all my efforts to adapt, hardly a day went by without me being in floods of tears. Luckily, Mrs. Rose never did ask me to do any cooking as now all my confidence had been washed away. I felt helpless and hopeless.

One day John came back from a job-hunting trip to Sherbourne and announced that he had seen a potato field a few miles back. With great excitement we set off on a raid to fill up the pram and then our stomachs. We walked and

walked. The afternoon light began to fade and the night chill
set in. There was no potato field. After a few miles John had
to admit that it must have been a mirage. It was pitch dark
and icy when we got home. Now we were truly hungry. How
we lasted seven months in a constant state of cold and hunger
I can't imagine. Perhaps our youth helped. I was still only 18.

I shivered by day and shivered more by night. Nothing could
warm up that little, old stone cottage with its thick damp walls
and its tiny windows. I eventually made curtains from my
headscarves. The kitchen had a porcelain sink and a cold tap.
The kitchen floor was just earth. Our poor little cat, given to
us by a local farmer's wife, could not understand the difference in good cat manners: yes, it was allowed to use the earth
outdoors for a lavatory, but no, the inside earth was not an
acceptable place for it. You try teaching that to a cat!

★

The Colonel was the bigwig of the village and we held him in
high esteem. It was our honour to be invited to one of his
cocktail parties. I was beside myself with excitement when he
personally came round to deliver the invitation.

What a contrast his home was to ours. Was it a castle? Was
it a palace? It was the grandest house I had ever been in. John
revelled in playing a young English gentleman. He acted his
part beautifully. I, on the other hand, was floundering.
Paralysed with my shyness and ignorance, I found it hard to
make any conversation. My discomfort sat on me like a dark
shadow. John was wonderful. My heart was filled with admiration as he mingled and chatted comfortably to everyone,
oozing charm and eloquence. There was a fantastic spread of
food laid out on a huge table in the centre of the room: small,

delicate sandwiches, delicious savoury pastries, asparagus wrapped in thin brown bread. It seemed as if it was food fit for the Gods. I was no God and I was so hungry that it was difficult to eat in a dainty, ladylike way. I managed now and again to put a sandwich and other goodies discreetly into my pockets for later. I was wearing a long sleeved cardigan with big patch pockets. I remember it was olive green. On the same table was a glass tumbler stuffed full of cigarettes. John had schooled me before we left for the party: I would take a cigarette and roll it up in my sleeve, then take another and roll the sleeve again. By the time we left my sleeves were rolled up to almost my armpits. I had been so clever, I thought. John and I thanked our host and left the party, both of us with our sleeves rolled up unbecomingly high.

"Well done," John laughed, hugging me.

"Careful," I laughed back, gently pushing him away. "We mustn't damage the goods!"

Once home we unrolled our sleeves over a tablecloth. The cigarettes tumbled out. They were torn to shreds. The tobacco was easily saved though. The food fell out of my pockets in a crumbling mess. We laughed and laughed. We could eat and smoke again!

*

Enough was enough. We had lasted seven long months but we were defeated. We packed up and left for London. My parents agreed straight away to put us up but they only had one single bed spare. John quickly found night work in an ice cream factory so I could sleep in the bed at night; as I got up in the morning, he got in. It was a practical solution but not an ideal way to live.

Thankfully this did not go on too long as John was offered a job at a prep school in Berkshire. Joys of joys, a cottage was to be provided for us. Was this going to finally be our dream come true? My standards had dropped so low by this time that when I saw what was to be our next home I believed I had arrived in heaven. Water ran out of the taps. Lights came on with the flick of a switch. We even had a decrepit old bath. Our sitting room fire had a back boiler and, if well stoked up, could provide a lukewarm bath.

Life was better but it was far from easy. I had stopped crying but John's salary of £90 a year kept us in the poverty trap and the house was hard work. It was a rambling old thing with no heating but lots of rooms and tiled floors to keep clean. One benefit was the good rail link from Paddington to Newbury, which meant that mother found it easy to visit. It was good to see more of her. I had missed her badly when we were in Dorset as her excursions to us there had been so understandably rare.

On one of her visits she brought with her a new friend called Cynthia. She was a delightful woman and I warmed to her immediately. Apparently mother had warmed to her a great deal as well because before she left she confessed that they had become lovers. Mother glowed with happiness and it was clear that Cynthia was able to give her the love that no man had managed to. I found out that Cynthia had planned to be a doctor but during training she started on drugs (morphine, heroin, anything she could get her hands on). Even though she hated men, she slept with them for money to buy drugs.

When I married John I felt I had slipped into a different world and that my new experiences changed me. Now I watched the same process happen to my mother. She became a much more loving and caring person. Cynthia lived in a delightful mews cottage next to the Dorchester Hotel. I loved visiting mother there. Cynthia shared this cottage with her ex-lover, Ebie, a Czechoslovakian woman who was incredibly wealthy because she had been married to a diamond merchant. Mother, Cynthia and Ebie became great friends and went everywhere together. They had plenty of money between them. When I would visit they spoiled me with marvellous luxuries. I first drank Earl Grey tea with them, ate smoked salmon and asparagus on dainty plates and, of course, there was champagne. I felt it was a dream world, a world that I cherished and absolutely loved. Those visits, while they lasted, took me away from the grimness of my own reality.

Their help was a very camp gay boy who adored the set-up. Every now and then they would snort a little cocaine. Cynthia had been a registered drug addict for most of her life. She no longer experimented with the cocktails of drugs that had previously landed her in the gutter or in a clinic; now she injected morphine in a controlled and moderate way. It wasn't long before mother was also injecting herself. Morphine transformed her into the mother I needed and wanted. She became free to show her love, her warmth, yet still retaining the humour I relished. My ignorance of drugs saved me from recognizing the dangers. I could feel light-hearted and happy when mother was on a morphine high, fearless to show my love.

They were a fascinating distraction from my everyday life. Visits there became highlights in my otherwise humdrum struggle. However, the greatest joy in my life at this time was Michael. He had grown into an adorable toddler, loved by all the staff at the school, as well as the boys. He would wander through the grounds exploring hedges, trees, stones and picking dandelions. This was truly paradise for him and for me. During our stint living in my parent's flat, every morning I had to quickly bundle Michael into his pram when he woke (usually at five a.m.) and take him for long walks so that he wouldn't bang toys on the parquet floor and wake the neighbours or annoy my parents. Here, he could play outside for hours, then run inside, his cheeks bright red and shiny with fresh air and excitement, clutching a bunch of weeds for me. This was a kind of happiness I had never experienced. It took over my whole body and I felt love ooze out of every pore. Not surprisingly, I was thrilled when I found out I was pregnant again. I excitedly planned out how I would tell John. Would it be romantic, over candlelight, with soft music playing? Or perhaps more Hollywood film style, over breakfast where I would announce, 'Darling, I have something to tell you,' and John would sweep me into his arms, smothering me with kisses. Oh, I could see it so clearly.

I decided on the breakfast scene. It was a disaster.

I could hear the anger in John's voice as he said, 'We can't afford to feed another mouth. What are you thinking of? Life is difficult enough.'

After those words he didn't speak to me for four days. I was distraught at his reaction and unsure how to respond. I wanted to restore our loving feelings so I rang mother and sobbed down the phone, pleading with her to help me get an abortion.

Thankfully, she was adamant this was not the answer. Instead she offered me a small, regular allowance. Mother also insisted that she would find and pay for an au pair. Now that she was with Cynthia money was no longer the struggle that it used to be.

I accepted Mother's offer of assistance. When I told John his smile returned once more, along with his love and affection. By the time baby Jonathan was born my mother had quite forgotten her kind offer, most likely as a result of her new habit. Not knowing this at the time though, I revelled in a blissful pregnancy, growing happier and fatter by the day.

Five

1953, with baby Michael.

Our postman found our next cottage. John wanted somewhere new to live; somewhere near enough so that he could still work at the school but far enough away that he did not have to be on 24-hour call. Our postie, Mr Rouse, came up trumps. Dear Mr Rouse, he was one of the nicest men on this earth. If only all men were like him, the world would be civilised, respectful and beautiful. He knew all of the houses from doing his rounds and introduced us to the cottage when it became available. The Rouses also ran the local post office and village shop. There were only three shops in the village. Sometimes the baker would leave a loaf on the cottage doorstep. Also, the butcher would look out for us, giving us extra meat on the bones for the cat. The goodwill of the locals meant so much to us both, even though we were too shy to say thank you back then.

We moved into Birch Cottage in 1957, four days before Jonathan was born. It sat on top of a hill with splendid views. Due to the incline, the water pressure was very erratic. It rarely managed the climb and gave up completely twice a day when the farmer a quarter of a mile away was milking his cows; I still don't understand why. This meant that our main supply of water came from a pump in the garden. I soon learned to prime and pump it. There was no lavatory so we were back to using an Elsan portable loo. It sat in the coal shed at the bottom of the long garden, backed against a shed wall that had several slats missing, allowing the wind to whistle straight to your bottom. During the winter the snow drifted in and covered the loo.

Despite this, I loved our little cottage. There were just two bedrooms, small of course, and a tiny kitchen. The cooker could be displayed today as a work of art; it was eccentric and dispensed electric shocks. It was necessary to wear Wellington boots and rubber gloves every time I used it.

Summer bees buzzed, winters passed and I felt as though I was drowning in the warmth of my own happiness. Yet, it was far from an easy life. We didn't have a refuse collection or milk delivery, for example. As we were living a quarter of a mile up a very rough track, no vehicle would risk the terrain. This didn't stop us. I enjoyed bumping Jonathan in his buggy down the road to collect the milk every day. Not so easy to overcome was the problem of getting rid of our waste. Pits had to be dug and refuse buried, realities which John resented intruding into his romantic dream of the idyllic simple life. The result of his reluctance was maggots crawling on the kitchen floor from under the dustbin. I would beg (John would say nag), 'Please dig a pit. Please, oh please, bury the rubbish.' The Elsan too, had to be emptied. No, it was not an easy life.

John disappeared frequently to the pub while I drew comfort from the children. I had never experienced this before and now I was wallowing in the joys of playing with my two beautiful sons. This nurtured me and I began to understand, just a little, the wonders of life and the part it was playing in my own growing up. Both John and I had been brought up in volatile families. He had gone to a private school in Plymouth. His father, Philip, was a newspaper photographer and was in Africa on assignment during and after the Second World War. His mother, Eileen, left him for another man, leaving John, then 14, and his brother, 10, on their own with just the housekeeper popping in once a day. John and his dad didn't get on at all and fought all the time once he was back. His father had a heart attack when John was 18 and fell into the fire. John pulled him out but he died in front of him. John said his home was always quite violent and he had seen his parents fighting, usually in drink.

All this made us both determined to give the boys a secure and loving childhood. We set down rules for ourselves when I was pregnant with Michael. Young as we were, we could recognise the damage in ourselves, both our insecurity and low self-esteem. It's easy to see how and why we were so attracted to each other. We recognised the territory, the mindset.

A kind woman we had befriended in the village decided to move away to be nearer to her family. When she was packing up she offered us her huge Victorian wardrobe: far too big for our small cottage. I suggested to John that we could break it up into different parts, keeping the drawers, and use the rest to rebuild the hanging space outside the kitchen wall to put the Elsan in. We spent the next weekend constructing our new lavatory. The sun felt warm while we worked, spring was well into its season. I was so thrilled that I would no longer have that long trek to the shed and could now slip out of the kitchen to the Elsan in the wardrobe.

Despite the improvements, this cottage was still not entirely

John's dream. It wasn't long before he burst into the house full of joy.

"I've found it!" he exclaimed, pulling me into his arms.

As he told me about this new cottage of his dreams his eyes looked into mine beseechingly. How could I shatter the hope that lay behind those eyes?

"All right, John, let's see this place of yours," I said wanting to please, wanting to believe.

★

A wild garden surrounded the cottage and an amazing array of weeds made it almost impossible to discern what actually was the cottage. We came to the front door and the giant rusty key turned slowly, grating in the lock. As the door opened the smell of damp paper and rotting wood overwhelmed me. Goodness, it was dark. Not really surprising with only one tiny window to light the small room. A huge fireplace gave off an acrid smell as we entered. John was beside himself with excitement.

"This is the sitting room and here is the kitchen," he gestured enthusiastically. "Look, no doors so we can still chat while you are cooking."

A room of the same size led off from the sitting room. The only evidence that this was the kitchen was an old porcelain sink, grim with grime, a tap sitting over it.

"Welcome home, darling," John hugged me.

He was so thrilled with this, his dream. All I could see was that this was my idea of a nightmare. There were three bedrooms, two on one side with a staircase leading up from the sitting room. From here there also was a door that led into what

I might kindly call a 'nothing space'. Two steep and worn steps led into this 'nothing space' which had a tiny leaded window through which hardly any light could come through due to how low the thatch came down at the rear of the cottage. I believe it is called a cat slide, and yes, our cats loved walking and probably hunting all over it.

I hugged John back.

"Well, darling, not quite what I wanted but it does have electricity and one cold tap ... not the basics I've been dreaming of but perhaps we could work something out."

My optimism was rewarded with many kisses and hugs. Seeing John so happy made me determined to make this cottage into his dream home. This wouldn't have been difficult if we had had money. We would have to do it with imagination and good friends.

Returning to the tour, John walked through the small kitchen to the opposite door.

"Oh look in here," he unlatched the door. "This will be my study."

It was yet another small, dark room with the obligatory small window. Light was obviously not a high priority. Another door led from the study and opened into another small 'nothing space' but this one you couldn't even stand up in. It was three and a half feet high. I suppose it would be good for storage if you didn't mind your stuff getting damp. A rickety staircase led into the third bedroom. All the downstairs ceilings were quite low. John could just about stand up but he did have to duck below the beams that kept the sagging ceiling up, and sag it did. The two rooms above that end of the cottage became our bedroom and the boys' bedroom. As the sagging ceiling below implied, the floor of our bedroom slanted and dipped. After we moved in we ended up putting bricks underneath one end of the bed and it would take me months to stop feeling seasick when I walked across the bedroom. The thatch was so deep and thick it took almost all the light from the small window.

As we finished the tour and came back downstairs my heart sank. This was yet another derelict cottage. John picked up on my disappointment.

"I want this cottage more than I've ever wanted anything. What can I do to make it better for you?"

He squeezed my cold hand and looked so deeply and lovingly into my eyes that I just couldn't let him know how horrified I was at the prospect of moving in here, into this deeply depressing, dark, damp hole.

"There is one thing I will insist on," I replied, knowing that he couldn't refuse me if he wanted this place so much. "Please put the Elsan indoors. I am fed up with always having to go outside in all weathers. We could put it in that nothing space off the sitting room."

John agreed at once.

An indoor loo at last, never mind that it didn't flush and that John would once again be on pit digging duty. Bliss! No more freezing, soaking wet walks to the Elsan.

On the 4th of November 1959 we moved in. We'd spent some days begging friends to help clean the place up. One of the most offending sights was the wallpaper. I'd never seen so many bold flowers printed on paper. We held onto pieces that had started to peel and curl down the wall and with great hilarity and a calling of 'heave-ho' we walked backwards, pulling the wallpaper with us. It came off wet and sticky only to reveal another layer, equally as ugly, underneath it. Altogether we counted 17 layers. Each layer was more and more difficult to pull of than the last. Hilarity dampened as we went hammer and tongs, scraping and scraping until the last lot had come off. We discovered beautiful beams that had been preserved under all that paper.

I insisted that every corner of the cottage was scrubbed and it was death to any spider that dared to cross my path. It was the duty of every helper to kill all spiders, and they did. Whatever made me think this blitz on spiders would last, heaven knows. The cottage had woods on two sides and a field on the other. The acre of garden was a haven for wildlife and insects. The cottage had sat empty for many years. The last tenant, an old boy who had worked on the estate, had drunk himself into a stupor. I gather he had done this regularly but one day he had a fall. No one knows how long he lay there or how long he had been dead. Not something I'd tell the boys until they were a little older. I was all for telling stories with a dark edge but not ones that could be blended into their real lives.

A lick of white paint everywhere was like waving a magic wand. How much lighter everything looked. Yes, I could make this into a really nice, cosy cottage. The next day was Guy Fawkes'. We took our sparklers outside, wading through knee high wet weeds, and let them off with much whooping and laughter. The boys felt our happiness and their spirits were as bright as their sparklers.

Six

Tough but Cool John.

Life together was not always as sparkly as that Guy Fawkes' Night. John was drinking heavily every evening. I had never known an alcoholic and didn't know how to handle the situation. I thought that I could avoid facing John's drinking by becoming the perfect wife. I never really saw myself as that but it is what I wanted to be. Domestic life consisted of desperate poverty, uncomfortable living conditions, no plumbing, and no heating. This adversity taught me how to cope. My time was filled with learning how to make do, finding the best ways to be thrifty and trying to make life as cosy and fun as possible for the boys. I was always busy in the kitchen and hugely inventive with the tit-bits that the butcher gave me under the impression that they were for the cat.

Meanwhile, I began noticing that John was drinking every night. He assured me he could handle it, as he never touched a drop of alcohol before six pm. I continued to avoid the possibility that his drinking was potentially a problem. Besides, John claimed that it was just something writers did. When George Barker visited, bottles appeared throughout the night and then disappeared as the two poets drank, sang and shouted. Sometimes drunken rows and fights would flare up. George was the only one who put John in this mood in drink. I would cower in a corner behind the sofa and pray that we would live to see another day; it was so violent and frightening. Eventually I learned that it was much safer for me to stay in my bedroom and let them get on with it. Although, on one occasion after a particularly heavy bout of drinking, George staggered off to the wood shed and returned brandishing an axe. Still, in the end no one was killed.

Among this alcohol induced drama we had some idyllic times. John bought a book on gardening and what with his efforts with that and mine with a cookery book; we had our own version of the Good Life. John did amaze me. I think that he surprised himself with his achievements in the garden. He spent hours digging and planting. With his shirt thrown down and his tanned body glistening with sweat he looked like a god. I watched him, lusting after him. Lady Chatterley came to mind. He was so handsome, so attractive. He looked like a 1940s film star and was my hero, digging to bring food to our table. As the sun went down John would end each day with the words:

"I'm just off to the pub. I won't be long, just a pint."

I always got a nice hug and kiss when he went out but I had to laugh. Not only would he stay out until the pub closed but a lot of drinking went on after hours. John was a good egg, a good chap, one of the boys. You could always be sure to hear a good story and have a good laugh with John around. He was everyone's friend and everyone wanted to buy him a drink. His popularity never waned. He is the only drunk I have known who stays a sweetheart no matter how much he's had. Heaven knows how he got home each night. He would fall through the front door still singing and laughing. He never got a hangover. No matter how much he drank and no matter how many people came to stay the night with us afterwards, John would be up with the birds. While the stopovers groaned he would make breakfast for everyone, the smell of sizzling bacon reviving the hangovers of the hangers on.

★

During this time mother's relationship with Cynthia came to an end. Ebie, the ex-girlfriend that Cynthia had been still living with attempted to commit suicide and ended up hanging on to life in a coma for some time. Cynthia cared for Ebie until her death but this burden took its toll on her. Overwhelmed with such responsibility and emotional issues, Cynthia felt unable to cope with her relationship with mother. Despite the heartbreak this caused mother, they were able to resume a platonic friendship a year later that lasted the rest of their lives.

When I looked at mother I thought she had lost her spark and her eyes were darker than their natural brown and like empty pools with no expression, no life. Gone was the mother I laughed with. There was no witty banter, no snide remarks at passers by when we sat in a café drinking coffee together. We sat in silence. I felt helpless and didn't know what to do or how I could understand what she was going through. Her pain and suffering was hers alone. Mother had lost the love of her life and at the same time decided that she would get herself off drugs completely.

I had no idea what a strong, single-minded and brave woman my mother could be. She was addicted to morphine as well as using sleeping pills. Going cold turkey the way she did reminded me of the film *The Man with the Golden Arm* with Frank Sinatra – watching that film was the first time I had heard the phrase 'cold turkey'. Father kept his distance throughout this time. He had moved out to be with his latest teenage girlfriend and when that fell through he managed to get a flat on the seventh floor of The Grampians, the tower block in Shepherd's Bush. Being so close didn't encourage him to look in on mother and see how she was. Father could not, and did not want to, cope with physical or emotional pain, although verbally he managed an excellent line in compassion. For months I saw little of mother as she battled on her own. She shut herself in her flat, drowning herself with loud music. Beethoven and Bach accompanied our telephone conversations. She spoke of the agony of the withdrawal symptoms yet she did not give in. Once she was clean, I could still see the pain in her big brown eyes. But this was the pain of her longing for Cynthia.

"I have got to do something, Esther, or I am going to go mad," she said. "But what can I do?"

Mother paced back and forth in her small flat, making it seem even smaller. Every day she visited her best friend, Ann Mankowitz, discussing what she could possibly do. In a moment of madness they decided to open a children's nursery together. That idea fell by the wayside, thank goodness. The thought of mother looking after little children brought me out in goose pimples. Then the idea of creating exercises began to take root.

"I don't know if I can do it," mother groaned at me. "I am not a teacher, I am a dancer."

Wolf, Ann's husband, encouraged mother. He was becoming famous as a writer (a film based on his book, *Espresso Bongo*, had just been released). Ann promised to be mother's first student and now that she was socialising with the stars – thanks to her husband's film – she could introduce Lotte's new, revolutionary way of exercising to them. The exercise world at this time was mainly comprised of a rigid form of army workout such as the Canadian Air Force exercises. The most modern was Eileen Fowler who had been Britain's first champion of keep fit and had devised her exercises in the mid-1930s. There was definitely a need for something new.

When interviewed, mother proclaimed how her unique workout couldn't fail unless you were lazy. The exercises were based on barre and floor work taken from modern ballet classes that she carefully redesigned for non-dancers. When photographed she would strike a pose with one hand on her hip, provocatively pushing it out to one side.

"Have you ever seen a flabby dancer? Of course not. They are firm all over and that is what I want to offer women."

As the sixties swung into life mother's exercise classes became the place to get fit and be seen. This was mother's moment. Pretty young starlets, writers, actors known for their serious work and celebrities known for very little, models and journalists all had a place on the green carpet in the basement of her infamous studio in Manchester Street. Mother fit into the sixties as if they were made for her. The miniskirts of Mary Quant made women rush to exercise their flabby thighs and bottoms. Fashion was dictating body shape and mother offered that body shape with her clever exercises. Biba had the right clothes. Sassoon revolutionised hair with his sharp cut styles. The new Lotte Berk technique gave you the figure. Mother had it all: the miniskirts and high boots, the Sassoon crop. She blossomed, every inch a Chelsea Girl. Fame flattered her spirit and the money and success that came with it gave her a lifestyle that she embraced with heart and soul.

I was excited by these days and happy that life had so much meaning for her. I wasn't ready to question my own life, though. I couldn't let myself see the drinking, the poverty, the struggle to keep our heads above water, the constant worry about our electricity being cut off. Occasionally it *was* cut off and the extra we paid to have it turned on again made me spitting mad. It was so tiresome to never have quite enough to meet our needs. What guilt I felt as the boys walked three miles to school in midwinter with nothing on their feet but plimsolls. I would line these with newspaper to try and keep the boys a bit warmer but it was futile, as the paper just got soaked. I did my best to overlook the facts of the hardships we were experiencing. In part perhaps this was a means of survival. Despite how difficult it all was, I felt a deep happiness. This was a real family life and I loved it. Now I knew and understood what a wonderful feeling of belonging and loving that a family could give. We were constructing the foundations that we all could grow from, and did.

It wasn't just me who, despite hardship, was finding a deeper fulfilment. Mother herself was blossoming. I was so excited at her new profession. As I watched her success grow it certainly never occurred to me that one day it could also be my profession and what all the consequences of that decision would be. As I now celebrate the 45th year of running my own studio I am so thankful for mother's exercises, which have helped me build such an interesting and independent life. I have met so many lovely people. I have grown in confidence and still enjoy my delightful students and the fun we have.

After Michael was born my figure, in its youthful elasticity, had sprung back to a nice shape in weeks. Not so with Jonathan. There was less elasticity in my muscles and they became far more relaxed with a second baby. When mother talked about her new exercises I knew I wanted to have a go. I needed them. By the time Jonathan was almost five I still had far too much flab for my liking. This was partly due to not losing the weight I gained while eating for two during my pregnancy with Jonathan and partly to my habit of turning to food for comfort after he was born. When John commented on how my legs looked like beer barrels I knew that I needed to do something. How clever of mother to invent her exercises and start her studio just when I needed it most.

As her exercises took off it was wonderful to see mother so happy and successful after her sad ending with Cynthia and her battle with morphine addiction. One evening she phoned me, her voice sounding full of life.

"Darling, I would love you to come and see my new studio, watch a class. Do come to London. I'll take you out for lunch. I'll send you the fare and drop you at Paddington at the end of the day. Please come, I really want you to come. I want you to meet my students, do say you'll come."

I was thrilled:

"Of course I'll come."

John was delighted to look after the boys for the day. I was thrown into a dilemma: oh what to wear? I had nothing that looked smart, nothing new since I was married. I wanted her to be proud of me. The hunt was on. Obviously I couldn't afford anything new. I went to a local jumble sale and was delighted to find an olive green pleated skirt with a Marks and Spencer label, a sign to me that this was a good quality skirt. It cost four shillings. Four shillings, which I am ashamed to admit, were scraped together from my family allowance.

Off I went to London, feeling grown-up and smart. I found my way to her studio. The class had started. I slipped in quietly and sat on the only chair I could see, beside an impressive desk with a phone and booking diary. I swelled with pride and wonder. This was a new mother, one that was different from the one that I had known. This was my mother the businesswoman, the exercise guru. Her character was even more flamboyant now, more driven, ambitious and outrageous.

I watched the class in awe of the speed at which everyone was working and the fun they were having. Mother's energy was exploding through the room. Her wit and sarcasm had the women in stitches. Laughter and adoration filled the room. After class was over mother introduced me to her students.

"This is Mrs. Fairfax. Mrs. Fairfax, this is ... "

She kept saying Mrs. Fairfax. I shook hands with the women, smiling, but I could say nothing. It felt so odd, as though I was just a visiting stranger. After her students left, mother apologised saying:

"I couldn't possibly introduce you as my daughter with you in that dreadful skirt."

I can't remember what we had for lunch. I don't suppose I could taste anything. Afterwards I stared out of the window as the train slid out of Paddington, seeing nothing, only feeling crushed, crestfallen that I had let her down so much that she was ashamed of me.

I thought the exercises were brilliant, though. I could see why they really worked. I wanted to do them so much. I think that it took another year before I dared approach mother about it.

"I really could do with your exercises," I said tentatively, testing the possibility of her turning me down.

It was as though that former incident had been forgotten. Mother was delighted. She kindly offered me a weekly lesson and was happy to pay my fare and take me out for lunch after class. So began a fun-filled time that would eventually lead to me being trained by her. Jonathan had now started school. I felt like a free woman, ready to begin this new career, unsure where it would lead but nevertheless filled with joy and enthusiasm.

Seven

Mother, Herbert her latest husband and me at home.

With Greta Garbo-style mother would frequently say, 'I don't want to be famous for my exercises. I don't want to be known as a keep fit person. Oh, how I hate those words: keep fit. I want to be known for my creative dance, for my artistic talents, to be taken seriously as an Artist.' She would raise her eyes to the heavens with arms outstretched in hope that someone would hear her pain.

As a Jewish-Russian refugee she could play this to perfection. She so loathed having the label 'keep fit' put on her technique. She felt it denigrated the exercises. They were born from dance, not the gym, and she would proclaim this frequently.

Even though she found it hard to admit, she loved her classes, her exercises. In her studio she found a stage where she could perform. Although she didn't value how she got it, mother absolutely adored her fame, revelled in it. When lorry drivers waved and shouted out, 'Hey Lotte!' as she walked down the street, she was in heaven.

Mother's wicked tongue and sense of humour attracted a cult following. Her classes became so popular that she ran seven hours of classes a day six days a week before she trained girls to help. I envied her stamina and energy. I never managed her strength, although I tried. Mother wanted me to live up to her high standard and I knew that I never ever could, not with the exercises, not sexually, not intellectually.

"Go hang yourself," mother greeted each student when they arrived at her Manchester Street studio. "You must always hang before we start. Only then are you able to warm up."

One length of the far wall of her L-shaped studio was lined with barres from floor to ceiling. When I arrived at class I would join the others in climbing up the barres, then holding onto one of the higher ones I would turn myself to face the room, slip my feet away from any support and hang. It was a good feeling. My body would stretch beyond any stretch I could achieve with my feet on the floor. Mother insisted on this.

"Hanging is essential for the spine," she would pronounce frequently.

Her word and her will were never questioned.

Manchester Street is lined with smart Georgian houses, mostly made into offices, each with black iron railings and steps that lead down to a basement servants' entrance. The entrance to mother's studio was like this only hers had been a milliner's factory when she took it over. When she moved in the sewing machines and most of the other equipment from the business had been left there for her to get rid of. Once she had done that her excitement at her new enterprise bubbled to the surface as she arranged for the barres to be installed, chose fitted carpet, had a tiny loo installed in a corner of the passage that lead from the basement entrance. No matter that the only window, and only chance for students to get some fresh air, was very small, facing a brick wall and fitted with iron bars to deter burglars. Being in the basement meant that most of the air that came down through this window was mainly fumes from the constant passing flow of traffic in the street above.

Over the years it is hard to imagine the number of sweaty bodies that must have lain on that green fitted carpet. How well I remember sweating on it as mother put me through my paces. Harder, always harder, she would push me, daring me to beat her. The stomach exercises were her favourite. Mother had to win and her competitive streak injected an awesome energy into the class. Such energy pumped through her tiny body. Her students would flake out, panting and exhausted, ready to enjoy watching the match of strength between mother and daughter. I always let her win. I would like to say that it was out of love and consideration for her but it wasn't. I was almost on my deathbed when I gave up and there she was, pumping away with a wicked smile brightening her face. Only when I had collapsed would she stop, to the other students' applause. This was all part of the atmosphere of fun that mother produced in all her classes.

After three classes in a row to Mother's four, I felt like collapsing. And she would then go on to teach three more the same day. Sadly, I did not inherit her remarkable stamina. Even one class could be crippling. Students would walk out of the studio with their legs shaking. When they got in their cars and had to change gears they wished for an automatic; their legs were weakened to jelly. The exercises were tough and there was something so satisfying about surviving one of her classes. I think that was part of the appeal. The other part was mother's wicked, and at times almost cruel, sense of humour. Frequently when working a position that was particularly hard to hold she would hone in on the first student that caught her eye.

"No, no, hold it. Don't move. Feel what's happening to your muscle. Tell me, did you have sex last night? You're looking a little tired. No, no, keep holding ... "

That was what made mother's classes fun. They were never boring. She ran us through the exercises at a pace that made your blood race through your body.

Lifting your bottom, stretching your waist, tilting your pelvis and folding over, over, over until your breath has deserted you. Standing at the barre raising your leg, stretching, bending, pumping. Sitting down with your back to the wall and lifting your legs, yes both legs. And what helped you survive these gruelling exercises was mother's constant verbal abuse that kept the laughter so loud I couldn't always hear the beat of the pop music we worked to. There was nothing PC about Mother's language; it was sex in every shape and form. Her thoughts about men encouraged the class to have their own say on the subject, which mostly seemed derogatory. This was a safe place to vent your feelings and of course he was never good enough, not in bed or at putting out the rubbish. As far as mother was concerned all men were useless, though she couldn't live without them. She had such a natural instinct to flirt, to play the coquette. How quick she was to bed them. How quick she was to throw them out. She was a natural predator with a killer streak. How men loved it, loved her. And so did her students.

Before long, mother became the talk of the town, attracting actors, film stars, models, celebrities and royalty. Television interviews, articles in newspapers, *Vogue*, *Harpers & Queen* ... she became the queen bee of London and attracted many stars and celebrities with her exercises which were so new, the latest and the hottest exercises yet seen. Although she was now in her fifties, mother was undoubtedly a woman of the 1960s.

She was often referred to as a diva. Fashion magazines wrote about her, intrigued by her cult following. Britt Ekland, Edna O'Brien, Sian Phillips, Prue Leith, Shirley Conran, Zoe Wanamaker and Maureen Lipman were just a few who came to her classes. I was awestruck as more and more famous women who were used to parading down the red carpet were drawn to the green carpet of the Manchester Street studio to be tortured by mother. And mother was becoming almost as big as the stars that booked into her classes. As her fame grew she was invited as a guest on chat shows. With her open views about sex, mother loved being interviewed.

"How is your sex life?" she would ask the startled interviewer.

This was her favourite question. She asked it frequently, almost to everyone she met in fact, and always delighted in the embarrassing squirm that resulted. Although the 1960s brought more liberated views on sex, it was still a subject that could shock. Mother loved to provoke and was always ready with frighteningly intimate questions. I think that the media soon cottoned on to the fact that they would up their ratings when mother talked about her sex life.

The more famous she became, the more outrageous she became. One weekend she was staying with John and I and we decided it would be fun to take her out to our 'local' in Newbury. We fixed it so that Olga, John's sister, would baby-sit the boys. John's brother, Barry and his wife, Liz, lived opposite the pub so they would join us there. A few more friends came along as well when they heard that mother would be there. She had quite a following locally, especially with our friends. As we walked in, the landlord, who we had known for a while, greeted us with great warmth and much hand-shaking with mother. I don't think I ever met a man who didn't want to shake mother's hand and a lot more, except for John. I think I married the only man who didn't find my mother a turn on. mother felt the same about John.

After all this handshaking, mother asked the landlord what his sex life was like.

'Oh mother, don't,' I whispered to her. 'This is our local and these are our friends.'

I was so embarrassed. I shouldn't have been. Everyone thought it was a hoot. As for the landlord, he reminded us of this moment every time we popped in. We never could forget it.

I felt so enlivened. I was going up to London once a week, working three classes on the trot with her. It was 1962 and I had decided that I wanted to train and run classes in Newbury, where I lived. Having trained as a dancer in my teens as part of my drama school studies, it didn't take me long to be good enough to teach the exercises. Soon mother passed me as qualified and gave me a Lotte Berk diploma. She dated it April 1st.

With all the time spent in the Manchester Street studio whilst I trained I started to notice a smell when I came into class and it wasn't just the fumes from the cars. I wasn't the only one who'd noticed either. Because the basement wasn't lived in, it had a damp smell. But now the smell wasn't just that. It was that mixed with car fumes and stale sweat, stale sweat mixed with a confusion of different perfumes. Mixing perfumes and stale sweat is a combination that is to be particularly avoided. Years and years of body sweat had soaked into the carpet and now it filled the airless studio (most of the time the windows were kept shut despite students' cries of desperation). The odours had nowhere to go.

Mother always knew where her popularity came from. It was from being down to earth, being outrageous, being herself. She said the studio wouldn't be the same if she were posh. She liked the studio unpretentious. But someone out there didn't agree. She was reported to Health and Safety. Of course they were horrified when they came to the studio. They were alarmed at the number of students mother could squeeze in. They decreed that the air was particularly foul and no one should be allowed to breathe it. The carpet was a health hazard and if it weren't removed they would have to close her down.

This interference pressed all of mother's buttons. At first she felt shocked, stricken and betrayed. Then her survival spirit kicked in.

"Is this how they think they can treat me? What do they think? They are behaving like the Nazis. What's happening to England? Has it become a Nazi state?" she ranted to everyone she met. To every friend she complained, "I came to England to get away from the Nazis. I thought this was a free country."

As she vented her anger to all, her accent became stronger and stronger. As always when she was angry, her beautiful brown eyes turned black. Snow White's witch comes to mind. There has always been something terrifying in her wrath.

The energy these feelings produced drove her to not allow anyone to tell her what she could and could not do. She spoke with people and found many students and friends who would be willing to fight to keep the studio open. It wasn't just that mother was adored but also that the exercises really did work and there was no way they would let her close down and stop teaching them. Mother was given addresses and telephone numbers of people who could do the work and do it quickly. Friends rallied and the next time I came up to London the studio smelled sweet, of clean air and fresh paint. A brand new green carpet lay pristine and sweat-free on the studio floor. Now, circling the ceiling right round the room, was a giant silver roly-poly cylinder. This monster was able to extract all that immovable, stale, sweat-ridden air and pump it out to join the fumes on Manchester Street.

Naturally everyone appreciated the cleaned up studio and classes continued to be as popular and as full as ever. And mother was getting richer and richer, too.

"I can't wait for you to see what I bought myself today," mother phoned one day, her voice full of excitement.

The next time I went up to London was a Friday. After the class, mother was bursting with excitement to show me what she had bought. We walked to the underground garage where she parked her car and there it sat: the Mini. It was black and shiny and so very *with it*. It was very much the must-have car, the must-be-seen-in car.

"Well, what do you think?" And, not waiting for an answer, she ran her finger along the side of the car, "Look, I've a gold line painted all along the body of it and my initials, LB, painted, discreetly, on each door!"

It suited her so much. It matched her jet-black hair, her deep brown eyes and her bright red mouth, a statement of confidence in who she was. I so admired her. Mother embraced black. Her hair, the car, and most of her clothes were black. Black and designer, of course. We drove her new Mini around London to St John's Wood for coffee and a cake. Then to Marylebone High Street for lunch and Holland Park for a stroll and to see the latest exhibition.

Thank goodness we often went out to eat when I was with her. Her diet at home wasn't my idea of nourishment. Her fridge was always bursting with chocolates. Occasionally I would notice a packet of salami, her favourite sausage. She had a sweet tooth, which some years later proved to be very bad news for her.

As mother's fame and popularity grew she trained more teachers – always very pretty young girls – to open studios throughout England and even in other countries. Although she had no sexual interest in these girls, she always had an eye for good-looking young women.

"Women are so much easier to get on with and such good company, it's not the same with men," she would state.

I never heard her say a good word about men. Yet what an outrageous flirt she could be. Not to mention how quick she was to get into bed with men. She was a coquette, luring men to fall in love with her and then, with the lightening speed and deadly intent of a cheetah, she would turn on them and crush their egos. Funny how some men, perhaps I should say *most* men, reacted to her killer instinct. They rarely crawled away with their tails between their legs, oh no. They would court her even more, declaring their never-ending love, trying to prove just how much they cared. This didn't do much for mother's declining respect for men. Her whole life, she only ever truly respected one man: her father.

More and more women wanted to train. Mother was de-lighted. She loved the idea of the Lotte Berk Technique open-ing up across London and the whole country. This was her world: the company of women, being the boss, respected, looked up to. It fed the needy child inside her, the vulnerable and dark side she hid from the world, although you could often see glimpses of it in her eyes. This endeared her to peo-ple, made men and women fall in love with her.

Soon, studios opened in Switzerland, Hong Kong, Italy, Malta, California, New York. Then, in the early 1970s, a young American woman joined the class, full of enthusiasm and flattery. Could she become a helper? She loved the exercises so much. Could she come daily? She couldn't do enough. She stayed and worked hard for nine months. She left to return to America. It wasn't long before this nice, eager young American was in all the papers: Callen Pinckney, author of 'Callenetics', the latest craze to hit the States and a bestseller. Funny, there was no mention of my mother. Yes, the exercises had a different slant to them but without being pedantic they were similar to the Lotte Berk Technique. Even the English press picked up the similarities. Mother was furious. Hot flames came from her breath whenever the subject arose. She was a dragon needing to roar at the injustice of it. She felt used, manipulated. Her wrath was so strong because someone besides her had become famous from her exercises. Later, in her eyes, I ended up being no different to Callen Pinckney.

★

My training days in London became the highlight of my week. I felt so grown up going on the train, being so independent. Not to mention becoming slimmer. Soon I had a very neat figure. I knew from first-hand experience how well the exercises worked.

I loved my day on the town. Not only because classes were such fun but also because seeing such famous faces in the classes – faces that I recognized – gave me such a thrill. We'd go out to lunch for a good gossip after we finished at the studio and then mother would drop me off at the station. The contrast between my day in town and my life at home highlighted to me our extreme poverty and how hard I had to work to run a home with no conveniences. We still had no plumbing, no washing machine, no vacuum cleaner and for some time I even had to iron with an old-fashioned flat iron that I would heat on the fire every few minutes. In London with mother I could forget the harsh life. We ate in nice restaurants. Sometimes I was treated to a shopping spree and my wardrobe began to acquire a girl-about-town look.

I so enjoyed our days together gossiping about her students or discussing her latest sexual encounter. Mother was always entertaining. We laughed together like a couple of teenagers. I enjoyed the break I got from the hardships of my life even more when I stayed the weekend with her. It was such a different life than my own. Saturday mornings would always start with the needle. She would slide it into her backside, a welcome shot of morphine to start the day. I knew that she was clean now but this had become her weekend treat, courtesy of Cynthia. 'Just a little something for the weekend' now had a new meaning for me.

Mother refilled the syringe, "Give me your bottom." She patted my behind and waited for me to pull my knickers down. "B12, that's what you need, you'll feel better for it."

She put two fingers on my bottom and rubbed. The pressure was meant to prepare me before she plunged the needle in. Mother had become an expert and she never hurt me. Was there a touch of morphine left in the syringe before she filled it with the vitamin? A part of me wanted to know what it was like, but no, I felt nothing. I knew she wouldn't do that to me. Mother then refilled the syringe with her own dose of B12 [a soluble vitamin] to give herself a boost. This became the pattern for my weekends in London. Mother was always in such a good mood after her little 'treat'. Much later, Cynthia, who supplied mother with the morphine, left London to live in Devon and there were no more such treats.

Mother got a real kick out of training me. I felt it, too. It was exciting for us both and seemed to unite us. Working together created a stronger bond between us than we had ever had before. It never occurred to me that the exercises that we both loved so much would one day destroy the deep friendship we were building. Mother had never been nicer to me, so generous and loving, even more loving than she had been when she was under the influence of morphine. I couldn't wait to start my own classes and earn money. I was still struggling to feed the family.

I applied to the local college to start an exercise class for them. I couldn't believe it when they offered me a hall in an outlying village. This was the beginning, oh yes. I earned 17 shillings a week for two hours work. Well, I had to start somewhere. My next step had to be driving lessons. John had been driving me to the hall on the back of his motorbike, me clutching the record player and records, in all kinds of weather. Driving lessons cost 17 shillings each. After a term, I asked the college for a rise and got 18 shillings a week. After paying for my driving lesson that left me with one shilling a week and I was still on the back of that motorbike. Something had to happen. Something had to change.

Before I had thought of training, before Lotte had bought her Mini, I was completely housebound. Money was always short. I spent hours cooking and baking. John had bought me a collection of Marguerite Patten's cookbooks. I have got a lot to thank for her easy-to-follow recipes. When my parents came down for a visit I'd set about making and baking. I loved the idea of spoiling them with something that I knew they loved and could never do for themselves. Cakes appeared out of the oven, tarts and pies. The house smelt like a real home and the boys could hardly contain their excitement and not only because of all the goodies that covered the kitchen table.

They knew that their grandparents would soon arrive laden with chocolates and sweets, things that were not normally available in our home. With great excitement the boys and I would wait at the garden gate.

"There they are!"

We waved frantically as they trundled down the road toward us. Turning into the drive, we'd run to greet them.

★

With my mother's success, things changed. After 30 years of marriage my parents divorced. Mother's bank balance grew and she was becoming a shopaholic. Even her politics were changing. Yet the one constant was that my parents stayed great friends throughout their lives. Having been through so much together: their flight from Nazi Germany, their struggle to survive in England in modern ballet (an art form that was only beginning to be appreciated), the death of my grandparents in the gas chamber, the experience of exile and making a new life in England and their shared past in Germany, bound them tightly. Not to mention both my parents happily leading lively extramarital lives. I remember my father sitting next to my mother's bed as they swapped details of their sexual exploits. The divorce, the disparity between their incomes, none of this disturbed their great friendship. Frequently they would go out together or come and visit us at the cottage together. Their crazy sense of fun forged a strong bond between them.

Eventually father married a pretty young girl. We were not surprised. He much preferred young girls, especially virgins. He had a real thing about virgins. This marriage lasted barely three weeks. His next bride-to-be was a schoolgirl of 16. He must have been in his fifties at that time. Her parents refused to let their daughter marry such an old man. But they were determined, although they waited until she was 21-years-old to marry. I think that we were all amazed that despite great difficulty they were together for 25 years.

Meanwhile, mother was like a magnet attracting new friends. She was training and opening studios, had trips to New York to open a four-story studio in her name. Money poured into her bank account and then out again. She was riding high.

"I think I'll have my eyes done," she declared one day. "I need a boost."

Many of her students were well known actresses who had these plastic surgery nips and tucks.

★

I get confused with the speed of my parents' lives. I think that it may have been the mid-1960s when my mother came to visit me one Sunday.

"Guess what I did yesterday," she teased.

"I can't, I haven't got a clue. Your life bounces from adventure to adventure at the moment. Come on, please tell me," I begged.

"I got married!"

Yes, that did stun me, shock me, leave me speechless. I also felt a bit hurt that I'd not been allowed to share this moment with her. I suppose I felt rejected, unwanted. The child in me felt bruised. I should have been thrilled for her but I just felt left out. I tried to say all the right things. Herbert was a really nice man, far too nice for my mother. He had been gently courting her for ages, begging her to marry him. He was 11 years older than her with a rather crumpled look about him, a stooped walk and, dare I say it, rather unattractive. But he was the kindest, warmest man you could ever wish to meet. I was truly fond of him, which made it even worse. After all, I knew what my mother could be like. He moved into her little flat in the Grampians. Luckily he didn't give up his own flat because within three weeks she had thrown him out.

After the marriage fiasco mother had her eyes done and was ready for the next adventure. I don't think that she ever loved Herbert, although I do believe that she had loving feelings for him. Their friendship went on for years. During those years poor Herbert frequently suffered her cruel tongue. Yet he was always there for her in her vulnerable moments, as was my father.

In the mean time I had been saving my one shilling a week. I soon learned that to survive I had to acquire a squirrel mentality. I rented my local village hall, just two and a half miles down the road, for an hour. By now I had gathered a few loyal students who agreed to come to my private classes – I no longer worked for the college. The rent for one hour was five shillings a class and I charged five shillings per student. You don't have to be a mathematician to work out how great that felt. I never looked back. Not long after that, I rented a room in Newbury, so now I had my own studio. The local television station gave me a great interview. A magazine called *Family Circle* that was in all the supermarkets at the time did a big spread on me with colour photos. I was building a reputation locally and getting myself known.

And that is when the troubles began. Big troubles. I never saw it coming. It was as though I was standing on a railway line with my back towards the train that was steaming towards me. Wham! Smash. Yes, mother was furious. She exploded.

"How dare you do this to me? How dare you. These are my exercises," she yelled down the phone.

I was bewildered. What had made me think she might be proud of me? I promised that whatever publicity I got I would be sure to say that these were her exercises. Now began an uncomfortable truce. Our relationship had changed, and changed forever.

Eight

1978, from my first published excercise book.

I love women: the good company, the camaraderie, the giggling girlie bit, the opening of hearts. Despite this, I have never found women sexually attractive, which is perhaps my loss. For me men make good bed companions; women make good friendships. In contrast, John enjoyed the company of men and felt more at ease with them. He had no difficulty in building strong relationships with men. One such friendship stood out as the strongest and warmest, that with our dear friend John Moat. He was also a writer. His company has always been delightful. Many a weekend he would spend with us at our cottage, the two Johns reading their latest work to each other long into the early hours. I took pleasure in their friendship, enjoyed listening to their latest poem. They frequently discussed the meagre fees poets would get should they be so lucky as to get a poem published or be asked to do a poetry reading. John was no longer doing any teaching.

First it was just talk, talk, talk. Talking led to a slow blossoming of something special. That something is the Arvon Foundation, the well-established charity for residential writing courses. The two Johns' dream of creating an establishment that offered people a chance to express their creativity grew into reality. This forum for writers to share their knowledge and experience, to pass on their craft and skills in literature and poetry was, indeed, a heroic venture where everyone involved benefited, and still do to this day. What started as such a small seed grew into a great tree with many branches. Arvon now employs many well-known writers and poets. This achievement will, no doubt, go down in history. And even better than posterity, whenever John taught a course he would get paid properly.

My classes also helped to put food on the table. Life seemed to be a little less of a struggle, although it was still not that easy.

"I'm fed up," I sighed one evening to John. "All this filling the tin tub for us to have baths and heating pans of water ... are we ever going to have decent plumbing?"

John had just emptied the Sunday night bathtub.

"I'm also fed up with being left to empty the Elsan when you're away," I went on in a disgruntled manner.

I knew that John felt the same way; it was a chore, a really huge chore. My words fell on fertile ground. Deep in thought, John gazed into the crackling fire.

"First thing tomorrow I'll go to the estate office and talk to them. You're right, it's time we had a loo that flushes and a proper bath with running hot water."

What happiness! We celebrated that evening by opening some of our homemade beer.

Our new bathroom was built into one of those 'nothing spaces' that many old cottages have, a space too small to be a room but too large to not use for something. Our wonderful landlord took care of the overall cost and our rent was put up by £2, which doubled the total rent to £4 a week. Unbelievable. It was as if an angel was taking care of us.

The boys were not impressed with the new bath time regime.

"But we can't watch television," they whined.

"And I liked it best bathing right in front of the fire," Jonathan complained.

No, they were not happy. I certainly was though. Oh, the luxury of just soaking my body in hot water, of dipping my head back to wash my hair, of just pulling the plug and watching the water circle and gurgle away. No more carrying the tub out into the garden to empty it. No more heating pans of water.

Just as things started looking up, the next drama crept over the horizon.

"I don't know what's getting into mother these days," I said to John. "I can't do or say anything without her turning on me. I can't seem to get it right. I try to please her and that seems to make her even angrier. I hate it when she is like this with me."

"She's jealous," he replied.

"Nonsense. I've never heard anything so ridiculous."

"She's always been jealous of you."

"I don't believe it. How can she be jealous? She's so striking, a real beauty. And she has a brilliant mind, the quickest wit. She runs her own successful business. Men are forever falling in love with her and now she is enjoying the attention of a much younger lover. No, darling, jealous she cannot be."

"Sometimes you are really blind. It's not your lifestyle that she is jealous of, it is your youth."

It took me another 30 years to realise that John was right.

★

I was offered a 10-week slot on *Women's Hour* explaining various exercises that women could do. Eileen Fowler had been their regular but now I was given a chance. My excitement and thrill at being on the BBC was overwhelming but was quickly dampened by mother's phone calls.

"You must say that the exercises are mine, use my name."

"I do, mother, every recording I say that these are your exercises."

Unfortunately, *Women's Hour* never realised this was so important and cut it out of every recording. Although I explained that to mother, she never believed me. She accused me of stealing her exercises.

"Do you want to take these exercises from me?" she screeched down the phone.

This really hurt so much as I have always felt that they are hers, and that I was inspired by her and also so proud of her, proud to be doing her exercises and sharing them with others.

A year later *Women's Hour* offered me another 10-week run. I would have been mad to turn them down so I accepted. But my heart sank at the thought of how this would hurt mother. I so loved the feeling of being at the BBC. All the radio guests were treated with respect and I always felt well looked after there. Just as the newsreaders 'dressed for the part' by wearing ties and jackets (despite the fact that they could not be seen on radio), I was asked to wear my leotard and tights to 'demonstrate' the exercises over the airwaves.

After that, a new health magazine was launched which asked me to demonstrate a series of six exercises for them to photograph. Oh Lord, what would mother make of this? The magazine came out bi-monthly. I was in each edition until, sadly, it folded. Maybe she never saw the articles; she never mentioned them. And yet our relationship was spoiled by her anger and resentment. By now she was opening studios all over the world and her clientele were the very famous and rich.

★

Despite the changes in my life and my growing career, my home life was still more important to me. I learnt how to make all my own jams, bottled all the fruit that grew in our garden, baked cakes and biscuits and avidly read magazines such as *Women's Own*. I wanted to be the perfect domestic goddess. Perhaps this was to prove to myself that I could be good at something.

The magazines that I read gave me a clear message about how to 'keep your man happy'. So, of course, I followed the good advice of the early 1960s. Looking back, I now see that those magazines were still depicting the ideals of the 1940s. 'Always have a meal ready when your man comes home from work.' 'Be sure to have makeup on and be wearing something to make him desire you.' Unfortunately, they didn't take into consideration how rarely my husband went out to work and that my life was totally different to that of the typical reader. I wanted to look good for John but this just made his jealous nature even more suspicious. I explained to him that I was following the magazine's guidance about how to be attractive to him. He reassured me, saying that he always found me attractive, even if I wore a sack over my head. This didn't feel like a compliment. If only he could have said, 'You're gorgeous,' or, 'God, I fancy you.' That would have gone down a lot better. What was lacking in those sorts of compliments was partly compensated for by the compliments that my home baking produced.

My parents were not skilled in the kitchen but how they praised my culinary achievements. That certainly drove me to do more, to do better. My father swooned over my marmalade. My mother preferred my gooseberry and plum jam. The cakes I baked for my parents' visits would cover every surface in the kitchen. And as they got ready to return to London mother would slip me a fiver and I would fill up their car with food parcels. During these visits mother kept her sharp tongue to herself. Afterwards she would phone to thank me for the cakes and then spend the next half hour letting me know how disappointed she was with me.

"Esther, you are not thoughtful enough, you're not sensitive enough. I don't feel you really care about me. All my friends can see how competitive you are and what you are doing to me. You have no respect for me." On she would go, in her low, menacing voice.

I always ended up in tears. John was so supportive at these times, always gentle and kind. He would repeat to me,

"Can't you see how jealous she is?"

No, of course I couldn't. Mother was establishing a fantastic reputation. She was frequently in *Vogue* and *Queen*. How could my small studio in Newbury threaten her?

I appreciated the love I felt from John and my children but most of all I wanted to feel loved by my mother. What could I do to make her love me? Being good at her exercises and carrying on her work obviously wasn't it. Cooking and baking did not lead to the warm and loving relationship that I craved. What could I do to please her?

I withdrew a little to a safer place, within myself. I stopped going to her studio once a week. Eventually, in 1970, I could see no way to restore our friendship. I decided to give up my studio and to no longer run classes. By this sacrifice I imagined that mother would no longer see me as a threat or as competition. I hoped that at last she would see me as her daughter, as her only child and we would be the greatest of friends once more. We would laugh again, gossip, shop, and have fun together.

Closing this door to a very important and enjoyable part of my life did not succeed in restoring my relationship with my mother. I became more and more sad, withdrawn. Mother turned on me angrily. Once again I had let her down. I explained to her that I had thought that she would have been pleased.

"Pleased?!" she yelled down the phone. "Don't ever try and please me!"

Of course what she said was right. We should never change our lives to please others.

Having no work meant having no money. I was stripped of my sense of achievement. I lost confidence. I began to question my purpose, my role in life. These doubts invaded my thoughts and swamped me. No one noticed this decline into a dark pit, least of all me. I hid it well from myself and from others. I was blind to life and deaf to my own feelings. Denial seemed to be a good coping mechanism and it worked, for a while.

Through a friend, I got a temporary job as a rep selling a revolting aperitif that masqueraded as a cheap version of sherry. I stood in my local Tesco's offering small tots of this truly noxious, possibly lethal, liquid to all that walked through the door. It was a laugh and the girls working there were a great bunch. It felt good to be out in the world again. Although I was offered a permanent job I could not really see this as a future career for me. John hated me working in our local supermarket. What would friends think if they saw me offering free drinks at Tesco's? He was really appalled by my argument that there was nothing wrong with trying to earn a bit of money. He ignored me. For almost a week he would not speak to me. Everything he communicated to me went through the boys.

"Could you tell your mother that I will be out this evening?"

"Could you tell your mother to please pass the cheese?"

And so it went on. The atmosphere at home couldn't have been worse. John only forgave me once the job was over and he knew that my days at Tesco were finished.

I couldn't seem to please mother no matter what I did.

I couldn't seem to please John.

Nine

A loving moment with mother in our garden, mid-1960s.

I missed mother, the lovely and fun side of her, her contagious humour and spirited wit. I reflected on our first and only holiday together as adults. It must have been in the early 1960s. I was finishing my training and ready to start out on my new career. Mother, having recovered from morphine addiction and heartbreak, was blossoming. She was thrilled at her own successes and that we could share in her work. There was love and laughter and fun in the air for us both. An old friend offered mother her luxury villa in Marbella. She invited me to share a two-week holiday there with her, maid included. I was so excited at the prospect of going on such an adventure.

And what about my family? I pre-cooked several meals and begged friends to help out. John had always made it clear that his only achievement in the kitchen was to be able to boil an egg and he stuck to this throughout our married life. The boys were no problem; as long as they could spend every minute after school playing football in the field behind the cottage and were frequently fed bowls of cornflakes they would be happy.

Mother and I landed in Gibraltar at sundown. Mother had hired a little Seat for the journey to the villa. Despite never having driven abroad and the falling darkness, she managed to find the villa

"You amaze me," I grinned at her in admiration. "You managed to find the right road to Marbella like you knew what you were doing."

"Which, of course, I didn't," she laughed.

The next morning she said, "Before we do anything I must check the water in the car and then we'll go shopping and stock up."

After she had taken the sixth huge jug of water from the villa kitchen to the parked car at the end of the garden I was feeling anxious about the car needing so much water. I mentioned my concern.

"Don't worry, I know what I am doing."

This didn't calm me as mother had no clue what was under the bonnet of a car. As she continued with determination to fill the car up with water I could not stand it any longer. I came out to see what she was doing. As I drew near I was struck with horror to see her filling the oil tank to overflowing with water. We called the local garage, fearing that she may have ruined the engine. A chap came out and eventually all was put right and the car ran perfectly once more. Mother agreed to leave engines alone in future.

"You may have a fantastic sense of direction, mother, but, my word, you are not a natural mechanic!"

Despite the initial hiccough, what happy, lazy beach days we shared in Marbella. We ate loads of fresh fruit, which was such a treat as I had not had such delicacies for years. We talked and laughed, played music on the radio, and danced. Evenings were spent playing gin rummy and sipping apricot brandy liqueur. Mother never really liked alcohol but this drink satisfied her sweet tooth. Every night, about an hour before bed, mother would swallow her Tuinal sleeping pill. Within 20 minutes she was delightfully drunk and promising me the world. She oozed affection and warmth. I wanted to stay in this bubble forever. One night mother urged me to try one of her sleeping pills.

"The feeling is just heaven, you don't know what you are missing."

I always refused and this irritated her.

"Please try one and share what I enjoy," she pleaded.

Eventually, one evening I gave in. The Tuinal was so strong that I only had a lovely feeling for a few seconds before it knocked me out. I knew nothing more until the next morning when I awoke, rather groggy, with a cloud over my head and a body that couldn't walk straight. Mother, having started taking them whilst on morphine, was already addicted to them and one tablet did not have such an affect for her.

"You have to keep taking them until your body gets accustomed to them and then you can stay awake longer," she assured me.

Mother loved it when we were both on a high. After a while I began to understand the pleasure of them myself. Once the pill started to work on you, you no longer had any worries, no problems of any kind. Life was sweet, wonderful, and nothing mattered. They became my magic pills. Once I was back at home, I asked my doctor for a regular prescription. In those days sleeping pills were frequently handed out like sweeties. They made such a difference to my life, not that my doctor allowed me to take the same ones as my mother. Tuinal was getting a bad name. Many famous stars were hooked on them. I was given Mandrax. Several years later they were taken off the market for much the same reason. Addicts used these pills as a complement to their usual drug of choice. For me they were perfect. They didn't knock me out but instead sank me into a relaxed state where no one and nothing could disturb me. It no longer mattered how late John came up to bed or how loud he snored or how many people he brought back with him from the pub or how loud they sang. I was at peace.

★

This holiday with mother had been the start of my long relationship with sleeping pills and led to a pattern of escape and denial. I soon learnt that the less I ate in the evening, the more effective the pill would be. The magic of my happy pill would work much better on an empty stomach. I also became afraid of eating too much at lunch. I wanted to get slimmer and slimmer. Now that I wasn't exercising, I was becoming obsessed with being slim. What I did not realise was that I was becoming anorexic. Despite my drive to lose weight I found it really hard to eat so little. I have always loved my food and enjoyed cooking. I came across an article in a magazine about something called bulimia. I had never heard of it before but it sounded like a better idea than starving myself. I would be able to binge eat and then throw it all up: perfect. Even as I write this I am disgusted with myself. Yet no alarm bells rang for me then. I simply did not recognise what I was doing to myself. I thought I was in complete control, it felt like I was. Of course, the truth was completely the opposite.

Even though I couldn't see it, I began to live a double life. During the day while the boys were in school I became increasingly lonely and felt isolated. After school I came alive. I was still able to have a good laugh with the boys, play rough and tumble with them, tease them. The fun that we had together kept me going despite the darkness that was always within me. Meanwhile, John was wrapped up in his world of writing, drinking and watching television. I started to take my sleeping pills earlier: nine o'clock, then eight o'clock. Now it was two pills a night. That was my escape. I could relax, drifting away from the real world. That way I didn't have to face how much John and I were becoming emotionally separated.

Our friends saw us as the perfect couple. We even fooled ourselves. No one guessed my secret bingeing and throwing up. No one guessed my addiction to sleeping pills. How could they have? We had not fallen apart. We appeared to be functioning like a normal couple, always warm, loving and affectionate. But it is not easy to fool oneself forever. Once I stopped the exercises, the downward spiral accelerated rapidly. Something was stirring deep inside me. I felt an irrational urge to run away. I had a desperate need to escape, to get into the car and drive, drive anywhere, to feel free, to run, run, run. I had to get out. I was not thinking of leaving John. I just needed some time on my own, some space, a chance to collect my thoughts. I arranged to stay with a girlfriend in London.

Michael was 19 and had recently moved to a flat nearby with his girlfriend. Jonathan was 15. They were perfectly able to look after themselves for a short while. Unfortunately, I wasn't. John would hold the fort whilst I had a little time out. All was well organised, or so I thought. I had not reckoned on mother.

"How could you do this to me?" she hissed down the phone. "You can be so hurtful. After all, I am your mother, how can you even think of staying in London with someone else when you should be with me?"

Mother was the very last person I wanted to be with. I needed time to think for myself in the care of a good friend who didn't need constant attention, who understood my needs. I had no fight left in me; I had sunk too deep into depression. I could no longer think for myself, a blackness of such density had enveloped me. I caved in and stayed with mother. It felt like I gave in every time. I had come to the end and had lost the will to live.

Mother's flat was not the best place for me. When she returned from her morning's work at her studio, she found me lying on the bed where she had left me that morning. She complained bitterly.

"You could have at least done the shopping. You could have cooked lunch. No, you just lie there and do nothing."

Mother was a survivor and believed in conquering the demons that visit you. Isn't that just what she had done? How often had she told me of her own struggles: being forced out of her own country, losing her parents to the gas chamber, not speaking much English, not finding work. I frustrated her for not being able to pull myself together. I could understand all that. After all, somewhere inside me I felt frustrated with myself. And yet I was feeble and helpless. She didn't know what to do with me. She dragged me out, believing it might cheer me up. She took me to her favourite cafes for coffee and cake, which I threw up as soon as we got back to the flat. I did the same with meals as well. I was throwing up every time I ate, far more frequently than I had been at home. I was spiralling down out of control. On one particular morning I woke up to find myself in the deepest, darkest mood. That day I walked through each minute like a zombie.

Mother took me out for more coffee and cakes, chatting about her classes. I heard nothing. The only positive thing I could do was to throw up. That evening mother had her young lover around. They were laughing and chatting and showing each other a lot of affection. I felt so excluded. Maybe that was what drove me to do something totally ridiculous and out of character: I got the telephone book and randomly phoned up strangers, chatting to them about how I knew a relative of theirs. I was very convincing. Each person I phoned chatted for a while until they became confused. I'd ring off then and phone the next random person. I repeated this again and again. My mother and her boyfriend laughed with amusement, enjoying my cheeky chats. They found this new 'me' highly entertaining. No one seemed aware of the speed at which I was travelling to my destruction. Only in retrospect is it obvious to me that every phone call was a cry of despair.

After the boyfriend left, mother went to bed. I went to the sitting room where my bed was. I sat down, staring into space, when my eyes focused on the bottle of whisky mother always kept for her lover. With little thought I unscrewed the top of the bottle and took a mouthful of the neat whisky. It burnt as it slid down. At last I could see a way out of my black pit. In a little while it would be over. I tried to crunch up sleeping pills in my teeth but they tasted so bitter. I tried swallowing as many as I could in one go, washing them down with the whisky again and again, one horrible mouthful after another. I stopped suddenly, remembering something mother once said. Anyone committing suicide should always leave a note to help the people left behind to understand. I fumbled as I wrote my note, my hands shaking. Already the whisky and pills were taking effect. Once the note was done I continued with the whisky and pills. I can't remember what I wrote. I slipped into oblivion.

When I opened my eyes I felt blinded by strong sunlight. I lay still, listening to unfamiliar sound and voices. I was shocked to find that I was still alive. No, that wasn't supposed to happen. I needed to die. I wanted to die. I looked through the bars of my bed, seeing nurses bustling up and down the ward. I was lying in some kind of adult cot. I turned to lie face down, not wanting to see where I was. My face felt the taut coldness of a rubber sheet. This could be the answer. In desperation I tried to suffocate myself. I must not be seen. I must be careful not to be discovered. I slid lower in my cot, covering my head with the blanket, wrapping the rubber sheet around my head but as I gasped for breath I found it impossible to go through with it. It was no use. I lay back and let the world take over.

"So, you survived," snapped the nurse who had come to check on me with a busy and efficient air. Her crisp, hard voice spoke to me angrily, "You are a time waster. We don't need people like you on the ward. We need the bed for people who are really sick."

And then mother came to visit. She drew up a chair, her face level with mine. Her eyes were no longer brown but black with anger. She lent in towards me. Her voice was husky as she whispered:

"How could you? Look at what you have done to me. I haven't slept. I couldn't even put on my makeup. I couldn't go to class today looking like this. I couldn't let my students see me like this."

How cold she looked. I longed for words of love, for reassurance. Perhaps she could touch me, squeeze my hand. She stood up and left with nothing more to say.

After a couple of days rest I faced an agonising visit from John, one that was awkward for both of us. Guilt at what I had put all my loved ones through joined my depression. Thank goodness the boys had only been told that I was ill.

The unsympathetic nurse walked me down to the resident psychiatrist's office, ushered me in and then disappeared. The psychiatrist sat behind his desk. He was a large, imposing figure. A beard like Freud's masked his face. Perhaps he *was* Freud. I can still hear his voice, strong and firm

"First of all: never live close to your mother. Keep your distance and stop allowing her to eat you up."

"Wow," I thought. "That is exactly what she has always done."

"And as for your husband, stop letting him use you as a leaning post, stop propping him up," he continued.

Of course, he was right again. I was not yet emotionally strong enough to put his wise words into practice. I never forgot what he said although it was some years later before I could follow his advice. In the meanwhile, once back home, I was trying to recover, trying to find a way to appear to be living a normal life. John walked on eggshells, trying to understand. So did all our friends. Mother found it hard to speak to me. As they tiptoed around me I felt more and more alone.

★

Mother would play the piano, with father accompanying her on the violin. I have such fond memories of times like that. I would stand behind them in the little third bedroom that had been turned into a music room. What laughter we shared when father's playing became a cat on heat or when mother's fingers, racing along the keyboard, would splotch and spill discordant notes into the air. I felt a part of it, included in the magic. We played gin rummy, my parents cheating as I would refuse to go to bed until I won. They only let on about that years later.

Father was an extremely handsome man. He always wore his favourite corduroy jacket and bow tie. When going out he'd wear his beret at a jaunty angle. Mother wore corduroy trousers and a waistcoat, her hair long like Veronica Lake's. Both my parents were great readers. Mother told me that she was reading Kant to me when I was 13 months old. The German philosophers were frequently quoted and Nietzsche was a favourite. Mother loved Shakespeare and said his language was like music. And, of course, music was an important part of our lives, both my parents having studied it. Whenever possible mother would take me to concerts at the Royal Albert Hall. If you went right up to the top, in the gods where there were no seats, you could go in for free. Mother and father were a striking pair in the 1940s. No one dressed like they did, in what was seen then as eccentric clothes. Women did not wear trousers except in films. Mother said that people would often stop their cars in the street to look at her. Both my parents were very left-wing. Father joined the Communist party. We had artists and intellectuals visiting the flat for debates. Sometimes they threw crazy parties where uninhibited sex was indulged in long before the 1960s.

Once mother became famous and had more money than she'd had since moving to England, she changed in so many ways. With success, mother changed her clothes to designer labels and changed her politics, even voting for Margaret Thatcher. Father and I nearly had a fit. Also, it seemed to me that as her fame grew, so did her cruelty. Her sharp tongue became livelier as she became more successful. Not just to me. Her sister Hilde got it constantly. Every man that mother was in a relationship with was at the receiving end. My poor father was whipped black and blue by her tongue, belittled, criticised. He never rose to these occasions, just letting her wind down and get it out of her system. I admired this so much because I simply couldn't do that. As soon as I was the target I collapsed in tears.

But now there was this dreadful distance between us. And although nothing was spoken, I could feel how anxious John was that I might have another attempt at suicide. He was right. I was mortified at my failure and had no interest in living, although I didn't dare even contemplate trying blatant suicide again. But, on the other hand, if it were an accident, yes, that would be better. Nothing nasty or messy like a car crash, I shuddered at the thought of that. Instead, I started to go out for walks on my own, exploring narrow country lanes, overgrown with bushes with bright red and white berries temptingly hanging down. They looked poisonous, deadly poisonous. I picked a few and ate them, wondering if the results would be painful. Overriding these thoughts was a feeling of peace on these walks. Being in my own space was such a rare feeling, breathing in the smells of nature, wishing life could always be quiet and peaceful like this. I didn't want to return to the cottage where life was suffocating me. And did the berries work? No. They didn't even make me feel ill.

Things got worse. John lost his licence because he was found drunk and asleep at the wheel, headlights still blazing. Unfortunately he had come to a halt in front of a police station in the East End of London. I had little enough space before John lost his licence. Now, when I went shopping John insisted on coming with me and I was never alone. He had always driven and hated when I drove (he was convinced that no woman should ever be allowed on the road). He had to suffer the double indignities of not only being driven everywhere but being driven everywhere by me. There was no space to breathe in my life. I felt more trapped and imprisoned than ever before. There was only one thing left to do. I had failed at dying, what now? I argued with myself.

"Well, if you can't die you have to live," a voice inside me surfaced with surprising strength. 'No one is going to come to your rescue and take you away from all this. You need to rescue yourself.'

With some positive energy running through my veins at last I decided to start up the exercise classes again. It was something that I was good at and it brought in some money and got me out of the house. But I had to start from scratch again. I hired a village hall in Hungerford. Four of my students came back. It was only one hour a week but that hour was precious. Slowly my confidence returned.

A friend of mine who used to come to my classes decided that she wanted to help me get back on my feet. She found a lovely first floor studio in Marlborough. She and her husband, with hammers, saws, nails and goodwill, built a partition in the room to create a changing room. The place looked so smart. A little advertising and spreading the word and I was ready to open. Mother showed interest in a more positive way when I told her about starting up the classes again. I was delighted and asked her to come to the opening party and say a few words and declare the studio open for business.

Unfortunately, when she came she was in a sour mood. She performed her duty. She coldly accepted the antique that I bought her as a gift of thanks and that I had thought might please her. I should have known better. She always did say, 'never try to please me.' Too late. She walked out and sat in the car. I had booked a restaurant for a post-party dinner for the family and friends who had helped make this all possible. The meal was silent and most uncomfortable. I was glad when it was over and mother returned to London. Once again, she ruined my success.

I, on the other hand, was delighted at getting my life back together, at being back at work. Classes were always filled with laughter and fun. The world had a better glow about it. I felt alive with renewed energy. Three days a week I ran morning and evening classes at my new studio. I also applied for a job in the afternoons at our local, newly opened, Health Hydro centre. They gave me work two afternoons a week. I met many famous and charismatic people there. One of them was the popular Katie Boyle. Her enthusiasm and warmth and lovely personality were utterly endearing. Katie loved the exercises. At that time, in the early 1970s, she was writing a regular column for the *TV Times*. She suggested that if I could put a few exercises together and print them in a leaflet she would write about them in her column and suggest that anyone interested could send for a leaflet with a self-addressed, stamped envelope and a 50p postal order. Wow and wow again! I had a huge response. I warned Katie that Lotte needed acknowledgement or she would get nasty but Katie had no such idea. Dear Katie, that was the name of her column, and dear Katie she was. She understood about family problems and refused to be intimidated by any threats that mother could make. The postman staggered down our garden path each morning. I could not cope with the amount of work that all this entailed and got help from one of Jo's friends, a delightful girl. All those 50p postal orders rolling in made me bubble with joy. John was thrilled for me and for the better living standard that it produced. He began to relax. Slowly, a better atmosphere filled our lives. I thank Katie Boyle for this, as well as for the important role she played in my future.

"Have you thought of writing a book?" Katie asked me on her next visit.

I had kept her up to date with the success of her leaflets and she was convinced a book was the next step. That evening after the boys went up to bed, well after nine as the boys were so much older, I prepared myself to speak to John. I felt tentative about approaching John with this idea. After all, he was the writer. I had no idea how he would react. I could not have anticipated his delight. He sobered up in an instant and, like an express train, ideas rattled out of him. He was full of excellent suggestions. He opened another bottle of wine. He was already celebrating, rejoicing in our future. And me, I felt overwhelmed with his pleasure and excitement. My life felt lit up from inside. I had better take an extra sleeping pill tonight. It wouldn't be John's snoring that would keep me awake, it would be all the adrenaline pumping through me. We felt closer than we had in a long time.

The next morning he was his bright self and full of how he would help me with my new project, suggesting that I get down to it and decide which exercises I wanted to use and in which order. He was going to type them all and correct my spelling and grammar. Now we both had a goal we could share and we worked well together. I wrote the exercises sitting at the kitchen table, trying to churn them out as fast as I could. As I worked I could hear John's typewriter going like the clappers. I tried to keep up with him but never could. Occasionally, he would come out of his study.

"I'll just make myself a coffee, do you want one?" he'd smile, patting my head as he passed me to put on the kettle, dragging on his cigarette as he went.

His study always had an airless, stale, smoky smell. Today it followed him out to the kitchen. I lit up as well while we had our coffee break and discussed how to structure the book. I was totally in his hands. I knew that he knew best.

"Next week we've got to get you an agent. I'll talk to Moat, he'll know."

And he did. Soon I was with one of the top agents at Curtis

Brown. Katie agreed to write the foreword. Her constant support gave me courage. It was all going too well. I didn't know how I was going to tell mother that I was writing a book about her exercises. Fear was certainly a big factor. I must have known that she would want to stop me but I was so thrilled at the idea of having a book out, a book that I had written, something that I had achieved. I just couldn't let the opportunity pass.

Ten

Mother with her Triumph Herald and first sports car.

When it comes to writing a book, frankly, I think that childbirth is easier. I frequently felt sick, sick at the thought of what I had started and the repercussions that lay ahead. It took nine months to write, re-write and read through the proofs. There were meetings in London. The publisher, Macdonald and James, accepted my book. They were well regarded and established. Nevertheless my fear and anxiety grew as things fell into place. Everything was going too well. The day was coming when I would have to face up to telling mother what I was doing and expose myself to her wrath.

John and our friends were incredibly supportive, feeding me with justifiable excuses such as, 'You have every right to write a book.' 'Naturally you will write a huge thank you and acknowledgement of her.' 'Lotte is already so famous with her picture in the glossies, her interviews on the telly, her studios opening all around the world. How can you be a threat to her?' But I was. How would I have felt in her place, I wonder? I honestly don't know. Friends insisted, 'You would be proud that your daughter was making a success with the work that you had established.'

Mother had been flown out to the States to open the New York studio. It was in a four-storey house in Manhattan with classes on each floor. She was feted and adored, and the studio became a place frequented by celebrities and film stars. The goodwill and support from my friends, my agent and my publisher in no way calmed me down; it only seemed to fan the flames of my fear. I do not know if I could have done it without the inspiration and support of Katie Boyle. She was the first person to say, 'You're worth something.' She helped me with her constant encouragement. During our chats on the telephone, Katie confided her own family difficulties. I had had no idea that other people had relatives that could be troublesome occasionally. It was good for me to hear Katie speaking so frankly and I was relieved to share my problems with her. Every time I saw her on television I felt a warm glow inside and I read her TV column every week. For me she was a real heroine and role model.

My anxiety about telling my mother seems to have caused me to forget what actually happened when I did. I do have a vague feeling, an emotional memory that excludes the actual event but captures the horror and the shaking that I felt inside of me. Although I cannot recall actually telling her about the book, the aftershock from it was unforgettable.

The bread was under the grill and a heavenly smell of toast filled the kitchen. Tea and buttered toast was a weekend tea-time treat at the cottage. I picked up the phone as it rang. How dare anyone want a chat just when the toast was hot and the butter melting into a translucent perfection? I did not want to be interrupted. When I answered, John knew by the sound of my voice that it was mother. He took over the tea-time ritual and left me alone.

"I won't be coming to stay with you this Christmas," she stated matter-of-factly.

The fact that it was only October and that we hadn't made any arrangements for the holidays yet seemed to have escaped her. I didn't ask why. No need. I had always been aware of her unpredictable anger but I had little idea how it would play out with the tangible stimulus of the book that I was publishing. Where and when would she strike with all the power of her wrath? As a snake's tongue darts brilliant and quick, so was my mother's next move. Not to be outdone, she had found a writer to write a book for her. This writer happened to be one of her students, so she understood the exercises very well and they had no trouble putting it all together and finding mother a publisher. She was fighting for her rights and I was going to fight for mine. The game was on and it was war.

"I'll agree not to make trouble if you hold back and let my book be published first," mother wheedled.

I do not know how I found the strength to not give in. I imagine part of me needed and wanted to assert myself in our relationship after being so passive and helpless for so long. At last I knew that I could, and would, stand up to mother. I refused to hold back my book.

The next thing I knew, my editor was on the phone:

"Lotte wants to take you to court and stop your book."

I could feel the noose tighten.

"It's your decision." the editor reassured me. "But we'll stand behind you."

As I listened I recalled the voice of the psychiatrist at Hammersmith Hospital saying, 'Don't let your mother eat you up.'

"Let her take me to court," I heard my voice say.

The editor didn't try to dissuade me or make a fuss. I felt a surge of strength flow through my veins. At last I was standing up to mother. I kept Katie Boyle up to date and she was encouraging and supportive, even offering to write a foreword. I could feel life switching into a different gear.

Eleven

Me excited with my first published book.

I was six-years-old. The big Victorian house we were living in scared me. It had dark corridors and dark corners. I was frightened leaving the warmth of the kitchen, the only room with any warmth in it, to go upstairs to bed. There wasn't much in my bedroom, just my bed, a chair and a chest of drawers. Heavy dark curtains (for the black-out) hung at the windows. One night after mother kissed me goodnight and closed the door, leaving me in total darkness, something ran over my bed. Scurry, scurry, I could feel its body as it ran. It was a mouse, of course. I screamed and screamed, the sound of my screaming scaring me even more. At last mother came in. The light from the landing lit a small part of my room.

"A mouse ran over me, quick, catch it!" I shouted.

Mother put the light on and looked everywhere. It was quite a large room but it had very little in it so it was easy to see all the corners.

"Nothing, I can't see anything. Don't be so silly. What, do you think that a mouse would be stupid enough to come into a house with ten cats in it?" Her voice was sharp with anger as she turned off the light and left the room.

I lay quietly in this darkness, breathing slowly and listening. It wasn't long before I heard the scrabbling noise of the mouse scratching somewhere nearby. I froze. I didn't dare get out of bed, so once again I screamed. I had to scream for longer this time. Mother took her time coming up. She marched into the room and put the light on.

"I heard a mouse. Really, really, I did," I explained.

She flung back my bedclothes, got a hold of my arm and dragged me to the bathroom. She turned on the cold tap and held my head under the water, slapping my head. Her anger was out of control. I was flung back into bed, dripping wet. Mother went downstairs and returned with a cat in her arms.

"There you are, then. Let the cat catch this mouse of yours," she screeched as she threw the cat into my room and shut the door with a slam.

Darkness, like the fear I felt, once again surrounded me. I must have fallen asleep eventually. When I woke up the next morning I saw that the cat was busy playing with the mouse. The creature had enough life left in it to try to escape yet each time it ran away the cat watched and then pounced. Its game of tease and kill was perfectly executed.

Mother came in. I hoped she was surprised to see the mouse after all that. Perhaps she was sorry for not believing me. I never knew. She picked up the wriggling mouse with one swift movement and took it to the bathroom. The bathtub was full, ready for mother's morning bath. She dropped the mouse into the water. It tried to swim. I went downstairs. When mother came down later she announced, 'I timed that mouse. It took 15 minutes to die.'

I recalled this little episode as the wheels of marketing my book went into motion. I knew how that mouse felt.

★

I had many good reviews when my book, *Help Yourself to Health*, was published in 1978. A book club brought out a large edition and magazines printed chapters of it. Foreign editions came out soon after this. I was offered a three-month regular exercise slot with the local television station. It was all such fun. Yet, I found it difficult to revel in all this publicity. The shadow of mother's spirit was like a cloud that hovered over me. When was I going to be put, like that mouse, into the bath to drown? It was bound to come.

Her book, *Lotte Berk Method of Exercise*, came out soon after mine. A polite veneer covered our true feelings. I went up to visit her and took a copy of my book for her, writing something loving and nice inside. We had a day of pleasantness and discomfort. She gave me a copy of her book in return, also with loving and nice things written inside it. I drove home with an uneasy feeling inside. When was the cat going to pounce? I got my answer a few days later in the form of a letter. Vitriolic words were scrawled across the pages in chaotic handwriting:

To Esther

Your last page in your book was so hurtful and full of lies. It made me know for sure how you hate me! I find it difficult to face you as our relationship is all pretence! You don't know what real suffering means. You are in your own country. You had a lot of help from me. You are so ungrateful as a person towards me. You are full of pretence you developed towards me and such utter ugliness. All I have is a deep feeling of sadness! You are a good taker! We have nothing in common as the past you made ugly! Are

you proud of this book? You gave me 39 years of happiness and what you became after that is alien to me!
The End of Mother and Daughter!

Mother

The end of mother and daughter! At first I wept and then I laughed. This was ridiculous. Had I instigated this appalling situation? What could I do? What should I do? Nothing made any sense. Unfortunately this episode dampened any enjoyment of my success. A shadow walked beside me as I smiled and chatted and signed autographs.

Mother and I didn't speak to each other for nearly two years. Part of me felt relieved to not have to put up with her angry phone calls. Part of me missed her. We appear to share the stubborn gene. Neither of us was prepared to talk things through. Isn't this similar to how wars begin? Both of us were suffering our hurt. For me, mother's behaviour had touched on my feelings of rejection, of not being wanted, of being useless, ugly and powerless. It took a time for me to understand her pain, her feelings of loss. She was fighting for survival, too.

Mother had had been forced out of her own country, losing her home, losing her parents, as well as losing her budding fame as a dancer and her family's fortune. She had been the youngest solo dancer at the Salzburg Festival. Once in England, she had to let those dreams go. She had been given the responsibility of supporting the family as it was hard for father to find work. Although none of this dampened her lust for life or for men. She had such passionate affairs, occasionally leaving father, always returning to his loving and forgiving arms when she had crushed her latest man. In 1941, she heard that her father and stepmother had been captured in Holland, along with so many other Jews who had mistakenly thought that it would be a safe haven, and transported to the concentration camps. Two years later she had to reconcile herself with the news that on 26 February 1943 they both had been killed in the gas chambers at Auschwitz. How did she cope with it all? It is hard to know exactly how her losses played a role in how she handled relationships. Is that why she always finished every affair, with the exception of her beloved Cynthia? Mother had to be in control and that went for her relationship with me, her relationship with her friends and her work. Now I was fighting back, refusing to be under her control. This may have aroused her many demons. I realised none of this at the time. In my eyes I was the mouse, fighting for my life.

Twelve

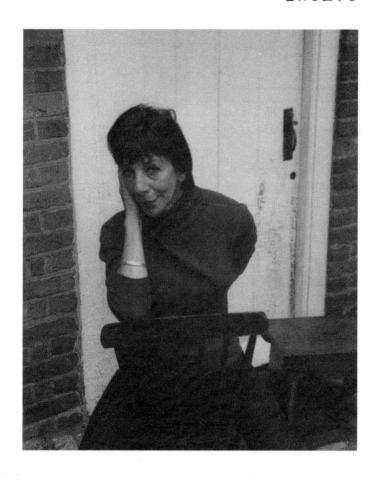

Mother outside our cottage with sex on her mind.

Like a fast running river, my emotions rippled through me. Entangled weeds wove around my feelings. Losing my mother, I had lost my best friend. Yes, strange as it seems, I did find that without the friendship of my mother I felt alone. When our friendship was good, even though it was always short-lived, it felt great. Now that we were enemies I was confused. Conflict left me bewildered. I had not learned how to fall back on my own inner resources. I didn't know that I had any. I did not yet know that the experiences that I was going through would one day make me a stronger person, a survivor.

I felt as if I was walking through all of the good fortune that came with my book without being able to be a part of it. I was unable to feel at one with myself. I started to write a second book, which another publisher had commissioned. Wasn't that wonderful? So much was changing in my life: recognition, money, and achievement. Why did I feel empty inside? What was wrong with me? From the outside everything looked good. Behind closed doors there was such bleakness. John continued to drink heavily. I continued to cut my evenings short thanks to my wonderful sleeping pills. I could not reconcile things with mother, yet I could not reconcile myself to life without her. And so life ticked through each day. I couldn't understand what was going on inside of me. Why couldn't I be happy?

The one area of my life where I did find happiness was with my sons. They filled my heart with happiness. But that joy was not able to spill over into the other parts of my life. I couldn't wait for them to come home from school, and later from art college. We'd laugh and chat, be silly, watch television. John would make us laugh behind his back as he shushed us while we chatted through the ads. 'It's the ads!' we'd shout and then fall about beside ourselves. By that time of the evening he had drunk at least two bottles of wine and a few whiskies. He would sink into the depths of his armchair in a stupor. Having the boys around helped me to see the funny side of those long evenings. The ability to laugh made it bearable.

Now and again I would receive messages from mother's friends telling me to stop being so silly. My Aunt Hilde tried to persuade me to make the first move. My father came to visit saying, 'You know what your mother's like. Don't take her silliness to heart. She enjoys her dramas but this has gone on long enough. Do what I do, don't take it so seriously, just let it go over your head.'

He smiled lovingly and motioned with his hand above his head. I knew that he meant it. That had always worked for him. No one understood that I needed to stand up for myself. All those years of mother moulding me into a clone of herself had prevented me from discovering my own identity. At last I was trying to be just me. Who was I? I still wasn't sure. I was sure that I was not my mother, nor did I want to be. I was also sure that I needed her to make that first move. If we ever were going to build a better relationship it had to be a much more balanced one. I grimly held out. At times I was glad for the silence and its peace. This alternated with sadness that the family was being disrupted and I seemed to be the cause.

I did not have anyone I could rely on, that I could open my heart to. There was no one that I felt could or would listen to me. I wasn't even sure if I could unravel the turmoil going on inside me whilst on the outside I appeared capable, happy and enjoying success. John was always loving and affectionate but if the topic of my mother came up all he could say was that I was better off without her. Meanwhile his relationship with the bottle deepened, as good friendships do. Our marriage had somehow split with the boys and me on one side and John and the bottle on the other. There was no doubt what his priorities were.

Meanwhile I was relishing the fact that our finances were no longer a constant anxiety. Nevertheless, I was still careful how I spent money; there was always a fear that it would dry up. John didn't want me to have a bank account so I filled up my post office book with as much money as I could. I bought him a decent second hand car, as well as one for me. Having my own independent wheels felt like a real breakthrough. My kitchen, which had previously had only the bare necessities and everything out on wobbly shelves, was given built-in cupboards. Oh heaven! A new cooker and fridge were installed. I also gave the family our first holiday. We went to Amsterdam. The boys had not flown before. I was thrilled to see their excitement. It was a truly wonderful adventure. It felt like it was the first time I was able to give us all something special to remember and enjoy together, and enjoy it we did. Maybe it was because John had to buy every drink while we were there, but he appeared to be drinking far less. Each day was such a pleasure.

Michael was now a very handsome teenager and wanted to discover Amsterdam without parental company. I tried not to be concerned, tried not to make him hold onto my apron strings. I realised that he was ready to explore not just Amsterdam, but life. What was the first part of the city that he discovered? Yes, the red light district. He also found the places where all the hippies hung out. He was growing up fast. Jo delighted me by not being ready to rebel, by still being my little boy. We enjoyed going around all the galleries together. The Anne Frank House particularly affected both Michael and Jo. Everything seemed so different: the canals, the bridges, the architecture, the cafes, the people. All of it seemed so new. It was different for the boys, different from their quiet, isolated lives in a remote country cottage. Over breakfast in our lovely old fashioned hotel, Michael would regale us with his last night's jaunts: the American student that he had met, the naked women he'd seen sitting in well-lit windows. It was so much more than a holiday. For Michael it was the start of his love for travel. For me, this trip showed me that I wasn't really sure that I wanted to go back to life as it was. For Jo it was a brilliant adventure, discovering museums and galleries and seeing new and fascinating places. For John it was looking forward to returning to the security of the bottle.

★

One morning soon after we returned from our travels a letter arrived in the post. I think that my heart actually skipped a beat.

"Oh John look, a letter from mother."

I hardly dared open it. Her very individual handwriting stirred a multitude of emotions. He gave me a reassuring hug, "Open it, it can't bite."

It certainly didn't bite. It was a brave and beautiful letter. Mother had always been very clear where she stood in the religious world: God did not exist. You were born. You die. There was nothing after death and nothing before. I follow that philosophy. For me it is the only thing that makes sense. In light of this it was quite a shock that she brought Yom Kippur into her letter. Having never had an education about my Jewish heritage I had no idea this was the season in which Yom Kippur fell. It meant nothing to me before then. It started to as I read mother's plea to forgive and forget, to start afresh. My heart soared. This was what I had been waiting for, what I had needed so much. I knew how hard it must have been for her to write those words. I rang her at once and arranged to visit.

★

The first time I drove up to see mother after this tentative reconciliation I lost my voice on the way. I thought I had laryngitis. It happened again the next visit, and the next. I thought it was just an odd coincidence that I only lost my voice on that journey. And then the penny dropped. It was my body's way of reacting to my anxiety about these visits with mother. Would she turn on me again? Was her anger smouldering silently and ready to leap out at me? The only way for my mind to cope with all my fears was to make me ill when I knew that I would be spending time with her.

We had started going out again for coffee and cake and nice lunches down the Kings Road or back to the Churchill for their delicious plates of salmon. Gently, gently we moved forward, both of us walking on eggshells. One visit, when we returned to her flat after an outing, mother checked her answerphone. There was nothing new about that as she loved to hear her messages. Only this time she looked to see how many but didn't play them.

"I won't listen to them now," she explained. "They will be from friends checking up to make sure that I am all right after a visit from you. They may be saying things that are not very nice about you."

Well, of course that hurt. She knew it would. How clever to put hurtful words into other people's mouths. How clever to manipulate it so that she was not involved but a mere victim. It didn't occur to me then that these messages might just have been pleasant communications from friends.

It took many months for us to relax with each other and to build a little trust between us. Although it was working in a way, it was never quite the same. Looking back on our relationship I can see how it was sometimes one of passionate love and at others, hate. It swung between these extremes, never stable. It was unpredictable and volatile on mother's side and withdrawn on mine. Humour was a great connection for us. Together we could laugh and laugh. Like that time when she took me to the Marie Stopes Clinic. On our way there, sitting next to each other on the tube, we had both lit up our cigarettes, placing them in our cigarette holders. We must have looked like such a couple of posers as we chatted and puffed. Suddenly I noticed that mother no longer had a cigarette in her holder. At first we couldn't see it. Frantically we looked and looked. We smelt a whiff of something burning. There in the empty seat next to her lay the cigarette, burning a little, smouldering hole in the seat. She swiftly picked up the cigarette, returning it to its holder. We fell about laughing helplessly. The arsonists of the underground! The people sitting opposite gave no sign of a smile. They just continued staring. We fell about even more, like naughty schoolgirls caught misbehaving.

And there was the time when we were off to Richoux, a restaurant renowned for its cakes. Mother parked the car. She held a birthday card she wanted to post.

"Oh, look there's a post-box. Come with me while I post this," she strode down the road.

We could see a smart looking man walking towards us. He wore a camel coat and had an air of confidence and wealth about him.

"Hello, Lotte," he smiled warmly as we met at the post-box.

Mother smiled coyly, "Do I know you?" There was a pause. "Have I slept with you?"

"No," the man replied. "I am your landlord."

Mother never said no to a one-night stand if she fancied a man. She was used to short-term amorous encounters so it was understandable that she had made this mistake.

"Mother, how many men have you slept with?" I once asked.

"I can't be sure," her voice was thoughtful and her eyes turned up to the ceiling in recollection. "I know that it is over a hundred."

Nowadays that may be more of a norm but back then it was unheard of.

I congratulated her.

"You didn't do too badly," I mocked. "And only seven abortions."

She shuddered at the thought of having eight children. We laughed and walked together, arm in arm, to her favourite M&S. She only bought food there, of course. M&S clothes were a definite no-no in her opinion. Their chocolate, on the other hand, was a favourite. Her fridge stood as testimony to her addiction; each shelf was filled with chocolate.

"I'm having such trouble with my teeth," mother complained as we lay on her bed watching television.

She was nibbling a bit of chocolate. Mother was well known for her sweet tooth and received lots of chocolates as gifts. She hated what she called 'posh chocolate'. The nearest she would come to it was M&S chocolate. Yorkie bars were her favourite.

★

1980 seemed like such a long year. Each day was a drag. Both boys had left home and were living with their partners. It was disturbing to feel so dead inside and still be living. How perceptive of Churchill to call depression his 'black dog'. That was what it was like. I could feel mine creeping closer, its shadow closing in. I questioned my state of mind. I knew that I did not want to die. But did I want to live? What would life be like in five years? The answer to that really scared me. I couldn't see any change. John and I would continue to sit in silent stupor watching television, a slow death for the rest of our lives. Things that I was unaware of must have been working beneath the surface. Earlier that year on a hot summer's day I began to have some very dark thoughts such as how life would be so much easier if John had an accident, fatal of course. I would be free, then. His drinking had not seemed to be causing him ill health. The only signs of his prolonged and heavy drinking were his 'shakes', which soon stopped after he had his first drink of the day. It was a wicked thought to wish him dead to get my own life back. Why didn't it occur to me that there were other ways of escaping an unhappy life without resorting to murder? At the time I saw nothing irrational in my thinking.

The garden was looking beautiful. The lawns were freshly mown. John was proud of his well-kept garden and flourishing vegetable patch, and rightly so. I felt the warmth of the sun soak right through my body as we sat outside in that idyllic moment. John sat with me, eyes closed, enjoying the sun. There was no sound except for the birds and the creaking of the tall trees that surrounded the garden. Was John having thoughts of how he could murder me as we sat in our own silent worlds? Probably not. He was a decent man. My dark thoughts, on the other hand, wouldn't leave me alone. The more I thought of him not being a part of my life the more convinced I was that I couldn't go on like this. Murder. Murder. Nothing interrupted this thought. Not the fact that my sons would have to sit through a court case and see their mother put away. Not the thought of the damage it would do to them to lose their father in such a grim way. No, none of the consequences of this dark wish entered my head. I must have been a lot sicker than anyone could have guessed.

One thought does manage to sneak in, a faint memory about a programme I heard years earlier on *Women's Hour* about bottling fruit. Suddenly I could hear the presenter's voice clearly, 'It is of utmost importance when bottling fruit that you sterilise your jars very conscientiously, especially if you have not included sugar in the bottling process. Botulism is a deadly poison that can kill and will occur if you do not follow correct sterilising procedure.'

Eureka! My mind sprang into life. It was only recently that I had bottled some gooseberries from our garden. I had not put any sugar in them, thinking that I would prefer to do that after opening the jar. Now, what if I had not sterilised the jars quite well enough? No doubt botulism would be present. The talk on *Women's Hour* said that it could take as little as 15 minutes before you died.

I opened my eyes to the tranquil scene around me, to the image of us in the sunny garden enjoying a quiet afternoon.

Even in my desperation the thought of me planning murder amidst all this beauty tickled my dark sense of humour. I leant towards John:

"Are you awake?"

John made a murmuring sound.

"Do you fancy a bowl of gooseberries for tea?"

"That would be just perfect"' he replied, signing his own death warrant.

I unscrewed the bottling jar and poured the contents into two bowls. I sprinkled sugar liberally over both bowls. At that moment, with no deliberate thought, I realised that I would not be able to kill John. What madness had overtaken me? I wasn't crazy, just unhappy. I returned to the world, shocked at myself. I knew that I couldn't serve John his fruit without knowing if there was botulism present or not. I decided that I would eat my own bowl quickly before he started to eat his, just in case. Well, I am here to tell the tale and John never knew about the murderous thoughts that consumed me that day. Plain unhappiness was a relief after being in the grip of such a malevolent desire. That episode made me sit up and take stock. I now had to admit to myself that I had to do something more constructive about my life. It couldn't just go on like this. I openly admitted to mother the depths of unhappiness I was going through. She kindly suggested that I go on a retreat and she would pay the expenses. I spoke to John and told him I needed to get away for a while to break free from these morbid thoughts and that I wasn't happy in our relationship. John was bewildered. He could see nothing wrong with our marriage but agreed that a short break could help me.

Nowadays it is easy to find a retreat offering just what I needed then but in 1980 the only respite care was in homes for the elderly. We visited a couple. The guided tour only depressed me more. I could not see how sitting around with a lot of old people all day would give me inner peace. All I wanted was to hide away from people and life, to be left alone. And so things carried on much the same. As October ended, the cold winds and frosts of November only mirrored how I was feeling. During a weekend with mother I admitted to my sadness and desperate state of mind. She offered to pay the first year's rent on a bedsit for me if I decided to leave John – but I wasn't to rush it.

Mother had decided that her lower denture was becoming a problem. She had been consulting a dental surgeon who promised that he could replace all the teeth in her lower jaw with implants. In 1980 this was not heard of in Britain. The consultant was a Canadian who had been practising this new technique very successfully in his native land and was ready to introduce his work over here. Mother was very excited. She didn't want me to think about leaving John until she had had the procedure and had recuperated. I agreed.

Returning home after having spoken with mother, the true depths of my despair hit me. Even though I knew there was now a glimmer of hope for my future, I still felt that there was nothing to hang on to. I was sinking into my lowest pit, drowning, helpless. I was haunted by a desperate feeling that I had left it too late and that I no longer had the strength to motivate myself to leave. Alarm bells began to ring.

John went away for a long weekend with the Moats in Devon. I had the cottage to myself. I stoked up the open fire. The cottage felt cosy and warm. My cat curled up on my lap, purring as I stroked her. The peace, the silence, crept through me like a warm glow. Tears slowly slipped down my cheeks. My crying turned into breathless sobbing. I put the cat down and paced up and down the room, hearing my crying, catching my breath for the next round of sobs. I couldn't ignore this intensity of desperation. Still weeping, I found the Samaritan's phone number. With shaking fingers I dialled it.

"Hello, Samaritans, can I help you?"

I couldn't articulate words through the overpowering sobs that still had me in their grip.

"Take your time. I'm still with you," his voice was warm, caring. I felt as though he was caressing my soul.

It was 10 pm when I made the call. By 11 o'clock I had started to become coherent. I explained that I couldn't leave my cottage; I couldn't even face living. He explained that it wasn't possible to get anyone round to see me until Monday morning but that someone certainly would come. In the meantime he promised to phone me frequently until then. And he did. His gentle, soft, reassuring voice was almost my constant companion that weekend. Without a doubt he kept me going.

I took the morning off from teaching class on Monday. I built a roaring, welcoming fire and put the kettle on for coffee. I paced back and forth in anticipation. What was I doing? What had I let myself in for? Could someone really help me?

I heard the car arrive and ran out to greet my new friend. And that is how tiny, slim, perky, bubbly Sue came into my life and changed it. After an hour's talking with her I realised that no one, absolutely no one, had actually truly listened to me before. For the first time, I felt heard. I was asked searching questions. I was allowed and encouraged to look at my situation as if I was an outsider. Was it really acceptable to live and feel as I did? Didn't I want more out of life? Wow. Now I had a lot to think about, rather then just dwelling on my situation. I had no idea that I had the power to do something to make my life better. Sue visited me often to begin with.

Slowly I felt a glimmer of hope for the future. My confidence, which had sunk beyond belief, recovered a little bit, enough to make me feel that life was worth living. I talked through every detail of my life and my feelings with Sue. She listened and listened. These were the first steps towards healing myself.

"I can't wait much longer, mother, I'm going to have to leave John and take up your great offer for rent," my voice was bright with anticipation at this big step.

There was an excitement in mother's voice, too. I was on the verge of changing my life and she could play an important part in that.

"Just wait until my operation is over."

"Well, okay," I was disappointed but I understood.

The operation was booked for January 5, 1981. This felt reasonable; I didn't like the idea of leaving John alone over Christmas, not to mention New Year. We had talked about a trial separation. In all honesty I didn't want it to be temporary but I couldn't be sure that I was doing the right thing until I knew what it would be like. Can we ever know the right answer when we are faced with life's challenging decisions? In preparation for the big day I arranged lodgings just outside of Newbury. The first big steps were being taken at last.

Thirteen

John exhanging cigarettes for a pipe. Smelly and horrid.

"It's so difficult," I confessed to Sue over coffee. "I feel I can't live with him and I can't leave him."

"You don't have to leave him. Perhaps there are things you'd like to change? What do you need from John? What does he give you that you hang on to?"

Questions, questions, wonderful questions. They made me face myself, the truth, and even better still, helped me to see that I could change my life. I realised that I no longer had to feel so broken, so sad, so helpless. Life is too precious for all that.

"Of course it's difficult," Sue took my hand reassuringly. "Whatever you decide, I will support you and be a friend."

It was wonderful to feel her friendship. I hugged her.

"Just a wobble. I'll be ok. Nothing is going to stop me leaving; it's my only way to survive." I looked at her.

"Did I tell you that I gave up smoking last week? I know it's madness to give up at this time, of all times. I suppose that I am trying to prove to myself that I'm strong, that if you want something, really want it, that is the best motivation, no matter what it is you want to achieve. I want to leave John and I want a better life. If I said to myself that I hope to do it or if I just rely on willpower it would not be enough."

Christmas that year was a farce. The atmosphere around the kitchen table was so stilted and grim. We still managed to work our way through the chicken and sprouts, pulled the crackers and built the Airfix model airplane that had long been a part of our holiday rituals. Then the boys left to go to their homes and lives, glad, no doubt, to escape the pain that was so tangible between John and I.

I didn't have the guts to tell John my honest feelings. We agreed that this would be a trial separation. New Year crept by. Time had never moved so slowly. To distract myself I started packing the suitcase I had set on the trunk at the end of our bed. I kept it open as a symbol of my imminent departure. On the 12th of January I would be gone.

Mother's operation was going to be performed at a private clinic in Bournemouth. Our last chat on the phone was loving and reassuring. She gave me the telephone numbers of the clinic and any others I might need to know.

"Have you heard of the grape diet?" mother asked.

"No, I don't think I've come across it," I replied.

"It's the latest and hottest diet. I bought a book on it. You know, you can even cure cancer if you stick to only eating grapes. I've done it for over a week now. My idea is that if I can lose some weight before I have the operation, with the few days when I won't be able to eat after the operation, I will have lost a lot. That way, when I come home I will be able to indulge in eating Danish pastries, lemon pancakes and some heavenly Yorkie bars. What a treat!"

What a lot of rubbish Mother believed in. The last time she weighed herself she was seven stone, six pounds, hardly needing to lose a single pound. But she was obsessed. I heard a voice in my head say, 'You can talk,' but I ignored it. I didn't have a weight problem. I had bulimia. We ended our conversation with good luck wishes and kisses. I felt an odd sensation of loss knowing that I could not contact her. The operation was a two-day affair, two hours at a time.

After the first part of the operation the clinic rang, "There is nothing to worry about, all went very well."

The next time the clinic rang, a reassuring voice told me that there was nothing to worry about but that mother had not yet come round from the anaesthetic. They asked me to ring later in the evening. You just know, don't you, when something is not quite right, an instinctual thing clicks in your brain.

"I'm not happy," I confessed to John. "Something has gone wrong, I know it."

"What could go wrong? She is in a top clinic with specialists taking good care of her." John gave me a reassuring hug.

His show of support was also revealing his need for affection as he clung to me. I appreciated his efforts to console me but I was not convinced. The day seemed to come to a standstill as I waited for the evening to come. At six o'clock I rang the clinic.

"I'm afraid that your mother still hasn't come round. We are monitoring her constantly and she now has 24-hour surveillance."

"What does that mean?" I asked, shocked at what I was hearing.

"Well, it means that we have someone sitting in her room keeping an eye on her."

I had assumed she would be attached to tubes and wires and high tech machinery with every breath being monitored on a little screen, the occasional bleep indicating any changes.

'Keeping an eye on her? What good is that?' were the words

that screamed in my head but I rang off instead of shouting them down the phone.

I turned to John:

"I think that she needs a lot more than an eye kept on her. We need to get her to a proper hospital with proper equipment."

I rang the clinic first thing in the morning. Mother still hadn't come round. Every alarm bell rang. I tried to hold back the tears and steady my voice as I insisted that she was taken to the nearest hospital. It was frightening how quickly the clinic agreed to this. No doubt they were glad to have her, and the results of their operation, off their hands. I rang again after a couple of hours. They told me that mother had been moved to Poole General Hospital. There was no time to waste. John insisted that he drive us there immediately.

The night before I had been so consumed with worry that even my sleeping pills had not been effective. I felt exhausted and terrified as we arrived at the hospital. I fought back the tears as it was explained to me that my mother was in a coma and in intensive care. I walked into the darkened ward where only the sounds of machines whirring gently as they kept people alive broke the silence. I felt cold and goose bumps tingled over my body. A nurse ushered me to where mother lay strung with tubes.

"I knew immediately that you must be Lotte's daughter, you look so much like her."

I looked at my mother, skin and bones, lying naked in this cot. A silent, hysterical laugh bubbled up inside me. Is that really what I look like? Oh dear God, wait till I tell her. We'll laugh about that for years to come, if we have years.

John was wonderful, more than wonderful. He drove me in to see her again the next day. I sat with her all day and they let me stay the night. The following day I stroked her skeletal arm and talked as much as I could to her, having been told this might help. Even though she was in a coma there was a possibility she could hear me, could understand.

That afternoon an extraordinary thing happened. A powerful energy seemed to take over mother's body. Suddenly she sat up and in German she counted, "One, two three," hitting the mattress of her bed with her palm. No one else would have known what she was doing but I recognised it at once. She was taking a class. She fell back on her bed, silent again. I had seen energy and life flowing through her. I went close up to her face and repeated:

"It's Esther, it's Esther," over and over again.

I was on a mission. I was not going to let her go. I am not sure exactly how many hours I repeated my name to her, my face close to hers, willing her to respond. Finally, I was rewarded.

"Esther," mother said, opening her eyes.

She also said a few other words that made no sense to me. What did that matter? She spoke! Mother was returning from her coma.

I stayed with her that night. As I sat with mother, keeping close, late into the evening a distinguished looking consultant came to check up on her. Had he been out to dinner? Had he broken away from a party? His perfect grey suit and white shirt gave him an air of someone stepping out of a society life. Mother looked up at him as he leant over her bed. Her eyes came alive. I suppose it was instinct for mother, the sight of a man put her into coquettish mode. She made some lurid sexual remarks to him. I could not tell if she was offering or promising those awful things that she was saying. As he left the ward I followed him out.

"I can't apologise enough," I said, horrified.

He laughed.

"I hear it all the time. It's not unusual, especially with old women coming out of a coma. They do say sexual things. It's nothing I haven't heard before."

He brushed the incident aside as one would forgive a foolish child. Little did he know that this was a normal sort of remark for mother to make at the best of times.

The next morning when John arrived he was amazed that mother's bright eyes recognised him. Covered by a sheet now, her yellow skeleton was hidden in a modesty she didn't display to last night's visitor. Mother couldn't remember anything about her ordeal.

"The only thing I can remember is a voice in the distance saying it's Esther, it's Esther ... It kept on and on. I knew that I had to get to that voice. You were calling me back."

Her big brown eyes appeared even bigger in her shrunken face as she looked up at me. I squeezed her hand and held onto her, so grateful to have her back again.

I went home with John that night secure in the knowledge that mother would recover. The packed suitcase still stood open at the end of the bed. Nothing had been spoken aloud but I felt that John seemed less on tenterhooks about the situation. Maybe he thought that going through the past few days together would have changed things. Maybe the fact that my obvious need for his help would make me come to my senses.

"Well, it's just her time of life," I once overheard him saying to a friend on the telephone.

I honestly think he believed that. Without any bad intentions, John had frequently put me down, ridiculed me, except for my cooking, he always praised that. How similar to my mother. I felt so invisible. The two people I most wanted to feel love from and to be valued by only seemed to appreciate my cooking. It's very odd in light of the fact that I felt so ignorant in the kitchen and always apologised for my efforts.

Both John and mother had a great need to control their environment, and that included me. Both were incredibly selfish in meeting their needs, although both often had good intentions. Mother could be surprising in her generosity towards me, especially financially, which I always appreciated. John was always generous with his affection towards me. Unfortunately neither mother nor John made me feel loved, wanted and valued. They just couldn't connect with my needs or show me the love that I yearned for. They did show me clearly how much was expected of me though. Where I went wrong was in trying to fulfil all their demands on me. I spent years trying to please them in the hopes of a reward of love. It is no wonder I became depressed, felt suicidal and had bulimia, all whilst juggling the role of happy wife and devoted daughter. No one guessed the turmoil raging inside until now, when I was finally trying to break free. Would this be the beginning of a new journey? Would I finally discover my self, discover life? Of course I would but I still had a long way to go.

The next morning when I arrived at the hospital mother was agitating to leave.

"I can't stand National Health hospitals, you have to get me out of here."

There was little point in trying to explain that it was thanks to this NHS hospital that she was alive and well enough to leave, that the care she had received and equipment they had provided had been of the highest quality and the best she could have hoped for. The fantastic NHS care was in stark contrast with that given by the private clinic that had operated on her. They did not have the facilities or the skill to save her life.

There, she hadn't even been put on a drip. All they had done was place a nurse in her room to watch her die. And they were denying that she had put £3,000 in their safe to boot. Mother was far too canny to be mistaken about that sum of money. If she said she put it in their safe, she had. Yet, in her snobbery she refused to recognize the quality of the NHS hospital that had saved her life and who, on her departure, returned every penny that had been in her purse when she checked in.

"You still need a lot of medical care," the nurse insisted when mother declared she was leaving.

She didn't want mother going unless it was to a hospital that could continue her post- operative care. Her lower teeth had only been placed in the top of the nails that had been implanted into her gums. These would need to be pushed down once the gum had more time to heal. I must say that at this time mother had a rather frightening appearance. She couldn't quite close her mouth and the teeth, sitting higher than the gum as they did, made her look more monkey than human. All this made it worse when the nurses instantly recognised me as mother's daughter because of our likeness.

"I want to go to the Clementine Churchill," mother announced "I certainly don't want to go to the London Clinic. The last time I was there was for my facelift and I was very disappointed with their service."

John followed her wishes and booked mother in for later that afternoon.

Dressing her made me realise how very weak she was. She was virtually unable to stand. Wearing clothes made her bony body look thinner than ever. A very smart tweed suit lost its shape as it hung off mother. We draped her mink coat over her shoulders. Nothing made her look even halfway human.

We arrived at the Clementine Churchill and I could see that

at last we were where mother could feel at home. London was her favourite city. And now she would be in this ultra smart clinic. John and I held her up between us as we entered the plush lobby that was filled with warm, welcoming lights, so unlike the harsh blue lights of Poole Hospital. A nurse came towards us, her makeup perfect. She had the face and body of a model and an embracing smile.

"Hello," she welcomed as she walked towards us. "Now which one of you is the patient?"

The next few days I spent driving back and forth to London. Mother's gums had healed nicely and her new teeth were pushed gently into place. Temporary cement held them there until the consultant was confident that the possibility of her body rejecting them had passed. Then mother was discharged, so happy to return to her flat. She was back, cosy with her TV and her cat, eating chocolates once more.

*

Coward, coward, coward. Like a Greek chorus, these words stabbed at my conscience. Yes, I confess, I was the very worst kind of coward. The 25th January, 1981 – this date will forever be stamped in my memory. That was the day I left John, left my home, left my two cats, left most of my belongings and walked into a strange new world. John had gone away for another weekend in Devon. Cowardly, I took this as my opportunity to leave without having to face him. I asked Michael and Jo to help me. I felt awful having the boys help me leave, for putting them in such an awkward, painful and difficult situation but I had no one else to turn to. I left with one suitcase and the television. I felt mean about the telly but mother had given it to me. The boys staggered to the car with it, making light-hearted attempts to lessen the sadness of the occasion. They saw me into the little furnished room I was moving into. To this day I have never asked them what they were feeling throughout this, nor what their thoughts were about the situation. Then I was left alone, a coward, a lonely coward unable to face the wounds I was inflicting on my family.

At least the next day I would be meeting up with Sue. I had been meeting up with her most days. Running my classes was also giving me a feeling of normality throughout all of these immense changes. Sue meant the world to me. I had never felt so close to a friend. I had never felt anyone outside of the family care for me so much. She was my first serious friend. We soon forgot about her role as a Samaritan. We laughed and chatted and put the world to rights.

"One day, Esther," she said in a serious tone. "You would make a great Samaritan. Leave it for a couple of years and then apply. Allow some healing time for yourself first."

This was incredible. Someone believed I could do such a responsible and worthwhile job well. I walked on air for days and repeated her words in my head. I could be good at something. I had to keep repeating that to myself. It was as if the winter sun was warming me through and through. Sue rang me one evening.

"We have to have a talk. Let's meet tomorrow and go for a walk on the common."

When someone says, 'we have to talk,' it's not going to be good news. My heart sank. The next day Greenham Common was white with early frost. We hugged as we met. For a while we just walked together, the frost crackling underfoot. The sky looked cold. I had a feeling that what Sue was about to say would do nothing to warm me.

"The director has asked me to stop seeing you."

I flinched. This was my best friend. How could anyone have the right to stop us from seeing each other? I was speechless. Sue carried on:

"We are allowed to befriend a caller but we are not allowed to let them become personal friends. That is what has happened. I'm not your Samaritan anymore, you don't need me in that role. I have become your friend. We have to break off this friendship."

"But couldn't we just see each other secretly?" I begged, not wanting to let go.

"My work as a Samaritan is the most important work I have ever done. I will be asked to leave if I don't follow the rules."

Sue held my hand, squeezing it through the thick gloves we were both wearing. I could feel her warm heart. I knew she had no choice. The Samaritans were her life.

I felt so alone again. I tried to control the sobs that my body wanted to release. This was such a blow, such a loss.

"I don't think I can bear losing you," I managed to croak.

"I promise you that I do not want to lose you either, Esther, but we have to say goodbye. Please don't try to contact me. This is how it has to be."

And that was that.

Fourteen

Mother with her beloved cat.

I'd never had a single life. There I was, 46, with no idea what to do or how to do it. Has anyone written a book about how to be single after 40? They should. The first thing I did was to find myself an amazing little house to rent in Hungerford. It was right on the High Street. When you went in the front door you did not go inside but instead came to a little white-washed outdoor passage that led to what looked like a doll's house. As you entered it there was what must be the smallest bathroom in existence with a bath made to fit a five-year-old. I soon learnt how to bathe curled in a ball. Beyond that was a dark kitchen with a small window that was too high for me to see out. An open staircase led up to a room with French windows that looked out onto a long overgrown garden, three or four times the length of this house. That was it, but it was mine, all mine. There was no furniture but friends rallied round. They found me a single bed, two canvas armchairs, a mirror and a small chest of drawers and I was settled into my one-bedsitter. Perfect.

It is hard to explain how I felt in those early days on my own. It was like I was a pendulum swinging back and forth between emotions. Sometimes I felt such elation that I would sit up in bed in the middle of the night and burst into song. Sometimes I wept so loudly that the sound of it made me cry even harder. My body struggled to catch a breath as I sobbed with desolation.

Each weekend I would drive up to stay with mother. She was still weak from her traumatic surgery but recovering. I would bring her several days' supply of homemade soup, which she devoured with delight. On one such weekend mother decided that she was strong enough to drive.

"Wouldn't it be fun to go out to eat? How about the FouTong? I fancy a Chinese meal," her eyes sparkled at the thought of it. "I can't wait to get my new teeth into some real food."

We drove to Kensington High Street in the greatest of spirits. After we were seated we lingered over the menu, tantalising our taste buds.

"We'll have an extra portion of bean sprouts for two, yes, Esther?"

I nodded. Bean sprouts were our favourite. We couldn't get enough of them and usually they were served in such pathetically small portions.

"Pile it on!" we said to the waiter, a sense of fun bubbling up.

Mother had survived her ordeal. I had survived mine. We were ready to enjoy the future and it felt like it was starting now.

Halfway through the meal an extraordinary noise gurgled out of mother's mouth. I looked up and was appalled to see that her lower teeth had lifted up on their pegs. Bean sprouts squeezed between her gums and the bottom of her teeth and protruded out of her mouth. The posts were part of the operation, set into her gum atop a silver horseshoe shaped device. The operation had been a success but it appeared that her body was initially rejecting these foreign bodies. She couldn't speak. She made grunting noises, trying to tell me to pay the bill and get us out of the restaurant. I briefly explained to the waiter that our exit had to be damned quick. As we drove home, mother was in a heightened state of hysteria. In her panic she forgot to take her automatic gear out of low. We crawled through the streets with mother's foot down hard on the accelerator. No matter how hard she pushed the pedal it had no effect on our speed. I kept my eyes straight ahead, not daring to look at mother, knowing the bean sprouts were still hanging out of her mouth. The engine roared as if we were on a racetrack and the noises that came spluttering out of mother's mouth belonged in a zoo as her hysteria and frustration mounted.

Once in the safety and comfort of her own flat mother went straight to the bathroom mirror pulling bean sprouts frantically from her mouth. Soon she was able to speak again. She phoned the emergency help line at the dental clinic and the crisis was over – she was told her new 'teeth' would eventually settle into place, and they did. My heart wouldn't stop pounding for the rest of the night after all of that. Bean sprouts drifted in and out of my dreams as I slept.

The following month, February, my first grand-daughter, Vanessa, was born. Michael couldn't have given me a greater gift than this new life as I started my new life.

In April the snow came and I was snowed in. Cosy and alone, I had to start learning how to be comfortable with solitude. I found this kind of aloneness more bearable than the aloneness I felt when I was living with someone else. Each month the pendulum swung less wildly. I began to make new friends. Curiously, although I did not go out to find friendships with single women, it seemed to happen that way.

Money was tight. I was now responsible for rent, electricity, council tax and gas. Our rent in the cottage had been a meagre £4 a week. These new responsibilities felt like a huge burden and I was scared, even with mother's help paying the rent for that first year. The salary from my classes didn't reflect the needs of my new situation. I got myself a job in a pine furniture shop that also sold attractive craft objects. I really enjoyed chatting to the tourists who came in but when it came to counting out change my neglected school years really showed me up.

"So, how much change would you like?" I would ask the customers expectantly. They were always so honest and obliging and would help me out.

As summer came I sat out in my garden breathing in the warm air and savouring my sense of freedom. I was settling slowly into my new life. I became more gregarious. I frequently chatted with my delightful bachelor neighbour. Sometimes we would share a drink and talk about what we wanted from our lives. Before, I would not have dared to speak to a single man. John's jealousy and possessiveness dictated that. This newfound freedom and this innocent friendship encouraged me to peep out from behind my shyness and play.

Fifteen

Mother & me mucking about in our garden.

"Are you more like your mother or your father?" a friend asked me as we sat in my garden one late summer's evening.

We had taken a bottle of wine out with us and a couple of chairs to sit in the overgrown wilderness that was my garden. The air felt as soft and warm as I did. I was relaxed, enjoying good company, even a drink. I had been anxious about drinking, afraid that any more than two glasses would send me down the road to alcoholism.

"What an interesting question," I replied. "I do have some of mother's wit and black humour. I wish that I had my father's brain. He is a real thinker. I have a similar body to his, well, with one major difference, of course. He's got good legs, so have I. He's got a flat chest, so have I. Both of us have wispy, thin hair." We continued sharing thoughts about our parents until the light had faded into the night sky.

Later that night, tucked up in bed, my mind pondered on our conversation. I have never quite seen myself as a drama queen, which mother certainly was, although, if you ask my friends they may contradict me. I don't have my father's nomadic free spirit. He was happiest in a tent or running around naked. Not I. His adventurous spirit was there even from the beginning as a young man living in Germany. After he passed his architect exams he decided to take his rowboat and his violin and sail around the world. When he started off the weather turned rough and his small boat was swept up by a storm. By good fortune he was thrown onto the grounds of a lighthouse. His around-the-world adventure would have to wait. He was truly a gypsy at heart, happy to roam by foot, bicycle or boat. Many years later when he was well into his fifties he cycled to Africa on his ancient, battered bike. In this I take after my mother who enjoyed travelling in comfort and style. What good sense. I think back to a summer holiday when once again my parents found it awkward for me to stay at home. I was sent off to the school summer camp. I was about 10-years-old. That was my first and last experience of sleeping in a tent. Everything seemed to get wet and stay wet. My sleeping bag companion had been a big fat slug. Nothing tasted good, nothing felt good, and nothing about any of that experience could in any way be considered enjoyable. Since that summer I have avoided walking boots, and hale and hearty men. There was one exception, though. Thankfully he understood my feelings and never encouraged me to join him in his favourite pastimes of running, walking, climbing and cycling.

I couldn't sleep that night for thinking about my father, of his many talents and his creativity. Mother always called him a jack-of-all-trades and master of none. She frequently put him down and belittled him. Was it his Buddhist leanings that made him such a tolerant and gentle man? He never rose to mother's barbed comments. He only praised her qualities, showing his love. I remember in my early teens he took me aside for a serious talk, telling me that he could never love me as much as he loved my mother. I think that he was honestly speaking the truth. Nothing that my mother did ever lessened that love. She slept around. She had seven abortions (none of them his). She threw him out, moved her lovers in, and still his love was constant. Believe me, I have not inherited such feelings of sacrificial devotion. Although, I suppose I didn't do too badly at that with John. I stayed with him through 30 years of alcoholism and poverty. Perhaps, after all, love has got such power.

My father was not an angel, nor a saint. Mother frequently called him a dirty old man. That wasn't far from the truth. Father, no matter what the age difference, preferred virgins. He certainly defrocked many of mother's young girlfriends. His seduction technique must have been sprinkled with fairy dust. Young girls adored him. He never had a problem attracting them. Of course, teaching dance at the college of further education, as well as running private classes, allowed him the pick of the crop. He met his third wife whilst teaching dance. She was a 16-year-old schoolgirl. He was in his fifties.

Later, father moved to Berlin where he had better prospects of work. On one of his brief visits to England we met up for a meal. Mother drove us to Fulham Road to get to father's favourite restaurant, Picasso's. We were enjoying the family outing. Father sat squashed in the back of the Mini whilst I sat in front. I twisted my body around to see him properly.

"How's your love life?" I asked him.

"It's not good," he replied with a wry smile. "There is this 43-year-old woman chasing me at the moment and to be honest, she's just too old for me."

"Father," I raised my voice in mock horror. "How can you say that, look at you, you are in your seventies!"

"Yes, I know, but I just can't get excited by a woman of that age. I want them young and firm to touch. Youth is so attractive."

"Well," I retorted. "Your love life is doomed. Of course, if you were a rich man that might make a difference. You still owe your bank over here £10,000 and who knows what debts you have run up in Berlin."

Father was always in debt and his Buddhist attitude didn't help; after all, what was money? It was a convenience and an inconvenience.

It seemed there were many different characters inhabiting my father. How many did I get to know? I knew he was a sexual man. I knew he could design furniture. We had some wonderfully unusual lamps at home that he'd made. His architect's eye produced ironic drawings of my mother's love life. His ear for music crossed continents: Chinese drums, African piano, Indian tablas, not to mention his mastery of violin, guitar and piano. He composed *musique concrète* before it became properly acknowledged. In 1947 he was the first person to introduce an Indian ballet to England. He learnt the language of Indian dance and, inspired by the movements of Indian dancers and classical Indian stories, he created the choreography of his own unique dances complete with dancers and musicians. That is how he learned to play the tablas. His fingers fluttered like butterfly wings as he drummed the hypnotic beat. I was mesmerised as I watched and listened. I learnt to wear a sari and put kohl around my eyes. The Indian women had such beauty, serenity and poise. I watched rehearsals as often as I could and began to learn the unique language of their dance myself. Every movement told part of a story. Rhythm came from everywhere. Musicians played on the stage, beating the floor as the dancers whirled with bells strapped on their ankles to accompany the music. The choreography in father's ballets was so far ahead of his time that they were only ever seen in small theatres in Hampstead or Notting Hill. It was mainly left-wing intellectuals and other artists that appreciated him. He was never going to make it rich and keep the teenagers he dated in style. They did not want a sugar daddy. They looked up to father in awe. He was their God and he loved it. He had such a following of worshippers. Mother could never understand it.

"I don't know what they see in him," she would say, her dark eyes rolled to the ceiling in mock bewilderment.

Mother refused to have sex with father for most of their married life. Eventually a precocious 15-year-old promised my father sex forever if he left my mother. So, mother and father divorced after 30 years of marriage. I was never told why his relationship with this young girl broke up after about a year. Still, no one could replace my mother for father and their friendship never died, despite all the adversity.

I certainly did not inherit father's attitude to money. He must have borrowed from every friend who fell for the enthusiastic sales pitch of his latest plans for a new ballet or musical venture. He only needed such and such, and they would cough up. His friends believed in him, so did the bank. No one refused him a loan except mother, who did so with great determination. With pleasure she would give him an earful about what she thought about him.

"You're like a beggar."

I remember one episode involving a distant relative from the British side of our family. I never quite understood how father met up with Curtis Berk. He was one of the British Berks, owning Berks Chemicals. I'm sure that father had a nose for opportunity and smelled money when he met him. It must have been the late 1960s. We were still living very much on the edge of poverty. My classes were not bringing in enough money yet to be of much help and John and I were struggling when father phoned me.

"I want to bring Curtis to meet you. He loves anything to do with the Arts and I think he may want to help you in a financial way."

John and I were beside ourselves. Someone with money who was a family member is interested in helping us? Time for John to open another bottle to celebrate. We couldn't wait for the visit. When Curtis Berk arrived, sophisticated in his well-cut suit and grey hair, you could see that he was wealthy. Quality exuded from him, even in the way he wore his clothes. I felt crippled with shyness. Father had mentioned what a cultured man Curtis was, frequently going to concerts and that he was a great lover of opera. I felt that I had nothing intelligent to say. John, on the other hand, was in his element. His Irish blood brought out the best blarney that I'd ever heard. I could see Curtis warming to him and loving the banter.

A few days after this visit a cheque arrived in the post with a lovely note from Curtis. He wrote saying how much he had enjoyed himself and that the enclosed sum was for John to buy himself a better second hand car, although he had thoroughly enjoyed the tales of all those breakdowns his present car had been giving him. We celebrated with much excitement. Things were looking up. John did use the money to buy a car. We felt posh and like we were moving up the ladder. I was not quite sure which ladder but it felt like the right one. It wasn't long after this that father came to visit. He took me aside for a quiet word. As we walked around the garden he lent in towards me, his voice just above a whisper. I could smell his breath and started to breathe through my mouth; his breath always smelled bad.

"I know that things have been tough for you for a long

time," he put his arm around me, his face getting closer. "I want to give you a small allowance. How would £2 per month sound to you? I know that it's not a fortune but it's just for you."

I couldn't believe what I was hearing. Was this really my father speaking, the father who never had any money of his own? The father who borrowed from every source he could? I melted. This was the most wonderful thing that my father could have done for me. I had long felt excluded from his care. This showed a love that I so desperately wanted. My parents were always affectionate with each other, even after their divorce, but I'd never been a part of this twosome. To walk around the garden with my father and receive this unexpected declaration of love meant so much. My heart flooded with love and gratitude. He was being a proper dad who wanted to look after his daughter. It was only money but it symbolised so much. I knew how hard-up he always was, his constant struggles with debt. Yet he still felt able to be generous to me. I was so overcome with thankfulness and deep feelings of love that I suspected nothing. I didn't smell a rat.

*

I had a restless night with my thoughts. I drifted in and out of dreams. The early morning sun reached my bed as it shone through the French windows. I sat up wide awake, my eyes looking out into the garden, focusing on the empty bottle of wine and glasses from last night's revelry. A tree stump had made a useful table last night but now it seemed out of place. As it was Sunday there was no rush to get up. I made myself a cup of tea and crawled back to bed, enjoying the brightness of the sun flooding my little room.

This Sunday I wouldn't be seeing mother. Father had driven

over from Berlin and was taking her out to lunch. This gave me a day where I would have nothing to do. What peace, what silence, what bliss. There was no one to answer to, no one to please. Today I would please myself. I made another cup of tea and went back to bed to enjoy the view through to the garden. Every morning the grass was growing longer and longer and the weeds were wilder and wilder. I didn't care, it was wonderful and it was mine, and mine alone.

As I sipped my tea my thoughts returned to Father. He would have left Berlin on Friday on his Triumph Bonneville, his pride and joy. How he managed driving through Germany and France on this great bike at his great age amazed me. I felt so proud of him. He was no ordinary man. He was a gypsy, a hippy. His long, thin, wispy hair hung well below his shoulders. Most of the time he wore it in a ponytail. Mother found this disgusting, 'A man of your age. You look ridiculous. I'm embarrassed to be seen with you, with your hair like that.'

Of course that never stopped her from going out with him, even when she ended up paying for the meals he invited her out for.

I thought back again to that walk he and I had made round the garden so many years before.

"I know it has not been easy for you, Esther," he had said to me, squeezing my arm. "And I have admired the way you have managed to look after your family. I'm so proud of you," he squeezed my arm again. "£2 a month isn't going to change your life but I know it will help." Somehow it had felt quite life changing, to know that some money was going to come in regularly.

Twelve weeks later the payments stopped. I was puzzled. I did not dare ask father why he had changed his mind about helping us, so I asked mother.

"Could you ever trust your father? Could you ever believe a word that he says? I was surprised that it lasted 12 weeks," mother shot these words down the phone like bullets. "I'll explain when I next come down."

And she did.

It turns out that Curtis had given father a large (although no one knows quite how large) cheque. He had asked father to give us a weekly allowance from this sum so we were not tempted to spend it too fast or too frivolously. But it was father who was tempted and after 12 weeks he decided to keep the rest for himself with no explanation to me.

Well, so it goes. I pulled myself back from these reveries and went downstairs. After breakfast I went out into the garden, finding it hard to get father completely out of my thoughts. All those years had passed and he still hid from his bad behaviour. It was as if he turned his back on certain events, which then never got explained. I closed my eyes and leaned back in the chair that had been left out from last night and which was already warm from the morning sun. I was chasing memories. I caught one. I was 12 and had started to grow very uncomfortable with father's insistence that when at home I should not wear clothes. As soon as I got home from school he told me to undress. Of course, he always ran around naked at home. Mother, keeping a touch of modesty, hated it.

He was adamant.

"It's natural. It's healthy. The body should be free of clothes," he would retort.

One night I was left alone with father. Mother was staying over with whoever was her lover at that time. I had gone to bed and was in that drowsy state before sleep takes over. I felt a hand weigh gently on my shoulder. It was father.

"Are you awake?" he whispered.

I murmured wordlessly, too tired to speak.

"Please come into bed with me. I feel so lonely without your mother. Please. Just for tonight," he continued to beg me.

Finally, I agreed, feeling that I should. I don't think that I would have dared to say no. The thought of standing up to others or standing up for myself made me curl up inside. I was used to my little single bed. His bed felt huge. All that room didn't stop father from coming up close and hugging me. Like an animal that smells trouble, I instinctively knew that something was wrong. I lay very still, hardly daring to breathe. Father gently parted my legs and placed his naked body over my naked body. His stiff penis pressed against my vagina.

With great gentleness he pushed against me whispering, 'Knock knock, who's there,' over and over again.

I have no idea how long this game went on for. I only remember his voice continually repeating, 'knock, knock, who's there?' and the heat of his body, the smell of his breath. He never pushed too hard and, thankfully, never entered me.

When mother came back home and we were on our own I told her what had happened; I could not keep it to myself. Mother listened carefully but said nothing, showed nothing. I wanted her to be distressed for me. I wanted her to care, to be cross with my father. It wasn't right that he had played that horrible game with me. I had hated it. I had been terrified, lying there so still, not daring to move, too afraid to speak, not sure what was going to happen. But she never said a word. It joined ranks with all the other unsaid things that littered my past.

Apart from confiding in mother that one time, I kept this secret for years and couldn't speak about it with anyone. Later, as I grew older, I heard about all sorts of other really nasty things that father did. Was I to consider myself lucky that it hadn't been worse?

It wasn't until I was in my forties that I brought the subject up with mother. I certainly was not brave enough to confront my father with this.

"Remember that time when I told you what father had done to me. Why didn't you do anything?'

"I was so angry," mother said, her face fierce with emotion. "I tackled him straight away with what he had done. I swore that if he ever lay a finger on you again I would leave him and he knew that I meant it."

Oh mother, why hadn't you said? Why oh why couldn't you have told me this? I needed to know that you cared and that you were angry and that father wouldn't do it again. I never knew that. I had to live with never knowing what he might do to me if we were left alone. Of course I did not say these things to my mother but those were the words burning in my head.

Mother then told me what father's response to her threat had been – 'I did it for her own good. I was teaching her the facts of life.' That is what he said. That is how he justified the unforgivable experience he put me through as a young girl.

Sixteen

Mother, always the flirt.

Adjusting to single life wasn't as scary as I thought it would be. I had always enjoyed my own company and for as long as I could remember I wanted and needed space to myself. After 30 years of family life the leap to single life was like flinging myself into the unknown. Perhaps that was the most frightening part. The convenience of the shops being just a short walk from my little house was a revelation, though. I no longer had to do a whole week's shopping at a time. I learned to cook for one and became ingenious at transforming leftovers into interesting meals.

Learning to live alone means you need to start having a social life. My social life when I lived with John was dictated by his drinking chums and their wives and girlfriends. When writers or poets came to stay with us a meal was always expected and I would play the gracious host. Now that I was single I had to take the first step and start inviting newfound friends around for drinks or a meal. If they only knew how terrified I was to cook for anyone. When I did, I felt exposed and feared that no one would want to come back again after their first visit. I wanted to apologize for every mouthful they took of the meal.

There were quite a few things that frightened me. I found meeting new people was always a terrifying experience. When I had been with John I had always admired his gift with people. He was such a warm and friendly person, one of the boys. His banter left people feeling he was their friend, a good sort. He entertained and amused people with his silver tongue and tall stories. There was always someone lined up to buy him the next round. I on the other hand felt shy and awkward when in a crowd. It was more comfortable for me to just smile in the background and leave the socialising to John. Now that life was different I had to make an effort. I had to learn chat and how to banter when I bumped into acquaintances. All those years observing John's easy going way with others came in handy. I said yes to every little invitation I was offered, knowing that later I could weed out all but the true friends that I wanted to build a relationship with.

As my independence from John grew stronger it was interesting to see how my own mother was becoming more and more dependent on me. She made it clear that it was my duty to look after her. I can still hear her words, 'It is your turn to look after me now. Daughters should take care of their mothers. When they get old, the children become the parents.'

Oh no. This felt so out of order. I had not felt taken care of as a child and certainly had no desire to mother *her*. It seemed incongruous that this woman who found it so hard to show love and affection now needed me. Throughout my life she had rarely let her warmth show. Now and again it had occasionally slipped out from behind a cloud and then it would disappear just as quickly. It was like this for the men in her life as well. She would let her warmth shine on them for a moment, they would fall more in love with her and then she would stamp on their egos mercilessly. Her favourite saying was, 'I'm going to make mincemeat out of him.' She would grind her foot into the ground with a twisting motion as she said this.

And now she needed my love. There was no one else, no lover to ease her neediness. One cold winter's evening we walked back to her flat after a meal. We were huddled together arm in arm against the icy wind. Her gloved finger began to poke at my hand. Poke, poke, poke.

"What are you doing, mother?"

"I am injecting you with love."

I could have cried. At last, in that odd moment, in an odd way, I felt her love.

★

The loneliness of my childhood prepared me for the loneliness of single life and it was not a source of fear for me. I had never made friends at school. The fact that I changed schools often made friendships difficult. I learned how to become happy and safe in my own little world. I could always keep myself company by talking to myself, a thing that I still do to this day. My best conversations are those I have with myself, without contradiction or argument, appreciating my own sense of humour and having a good laugh at my own witticisms and with no small talk, thank goodness. The ability to entertain myself from my earliest years was a gift that held me in good stead. And now I didn't need to dress up in my mother's clothes to go to the cinema as I did all those years ago.

At 47 I found those inner resources again. To be frank, they had been called upon quite a bit throughout the difficult years of poverty and solitude within my married life. Somehow this was different though. My frames of reference had changed and I had to almost reinvent myself. No longer could I retreat behind the powerful characters of my mother or my husband. I had to make my own place in the world, learn to make friends and shape my life as I wanted it to be. I was still haunted by the sadness of losing Sue, my first real friend. I tried to put it behind me but it was hard to. I looked forward to the opportunity of new friends on the horizon.

One day the phone rang. I was thrilled, not many people knew my number.

"Hello?"

It was one of my students. She invited me to a party.

"Yes, I would love to, thank you so much. Please do send me very good directions as I have a bit of a problem with navigation."

I give her my address and she promised to send very detailed instructions. When we hung up I jumped up and down, my cheeks flushed with joy. A party! I've been invited to a party, a champagne and strawberry party! I was so excited, my first invitation to a party! All day long I sang, 'the sun has got his hat on, hip hip hooray ...' It's party time for me! I must phone mother.

Before I knew it, tonight's the night. I was so scared. I would have to drive myself to Oxford. John hated women drivers, so he used to drive me everywhere. I didn't get my driving licence until I was 29 and then it was to his great disapproval. My nerves at the prospect of navigating my way to the party by car made adrenalin shoot through my body. My hands shook and my knees knocked. I really don't want to go, after all. I can't do this. Yet from somewhere deep within, another voice told me, 'Yes, you can do this. You must.' And so I did. The glow of an early summer's evening helped me find my way. Thank goodness it wasn't dark yet. Of course I knew it would be on the way back but I reminded myself that it did-n't matter if I got lost when I was homeward bound. After a couple of wrong turnings, my shaking hands were joined by butterflies in my stomach. The house was in a small back street with cars parked down both sides. Slowly I crept down it, searching. Yes, there was a parking space. By the time I rang the doorbell my legs felt so weak and wobbly that I was not sure if I would be able to walk in. The door opened, a glass of champagne was placed in my hand, and, after a hug and a warm welcome, I was left to mingle with the other guests on my own. There seemed to be a lot of young and rather trendy people in little clusters. They laughed and chatted and knew each other. What the hell was I doing here? I felt so out of place. I didn't seem to be able to break into any likely looking groups or engage with any friendly, chatting people. My glass was filled with more champagne. My hostess encouraged me to mingle. I became even shyer. I wanted to make my excuses and leave. I knew that I couldn't, that it was far too early. Bowls of strawberries were passed around. I wasn't interested. I couldn't seem to make my taste buds accept that champagne and strawberries were a pleasant mixture. Although, I must admit, I was quite happy with the champagne. If only there were other nibbles out, a little cheese or a bit of bread to soak up the alcohol. The music in the background sounded dull and old-fashioned. The record player sat on the floor with a pile of LPs next to it. I decided to examine what music was available, so at least I wouldn't feel so spare and alone. I crouched down and slowly went through the dreary collection. Soon I became aware of a pair of men's shoes just beside me. I looked up. There stood a man, on his own.

"I'm just seeing if there's more lively music here'" I ex-plained, quickly standing up.

Blue eyes smiled at me. He had a friendly smile, warm and

welcoming me into conversation. This was not the best time to be lost for words. I desperately searched for something interesting to say. Only a few banal words came out. My eyes took in his broad shoulders, blond hair and that amazing smile as we finally exchanged words. What words? I said something about my work at the health farm in Kinbury where I was teaching the Lotte Berk Technique two days a week. Where are my flirting skills when I need them? Buried under years of married life, that is where they were. I was not sure if he was flirting with me or not. I didn't pick up any signals from behind his smile and pleasant conversation. Was he just being polite? Whatever was happening between us, it was nice and I did not want it to stop.

A frumpy girl with mousy permed hair came up to him. She was about 36, could do with some exercise, not fat but plumpish, flabby. She wore a knitted acrylic cardigan twin set and pearls, not real. I took all this in with a moment's appraisal. She certainly wasn't right for him. Her sulky face fitted the whine in her voice:

"I'm bored, I want to go now. You knew I didn't want to come in the first place."

"Alright, we'll leave if you want to. Just give me a minute." I can see that he doesn't want to leave. He responds to her like a man who is used to being nagged. I sense his embarrassment. "It has been so nice chatting to you," he says, his blue eyes smiling down at me. I can feel them in my heart.

She placed a territorial hand on his arm and I could see how she was gently putting pressure on it with her hands as she pulled him towards her. She did not bother to smile at me. As they walked away I could just catch the sound of him whispering to her in irritation. Miss Sulky was leaving with the only person who chatted with me the whole evening. Not much point in me staying now. I picked up a strawberry as I walked out of the front door.

There was a spring in my step that lasted for almost a week. I had been to my first party as a single woman, which was a big step. But mainly it was because I could still feel the thrill of his blue eyes. These were the first signs that a new life was really beginning for me, no matter that the evening didn't come to anything. I was dusting and cleaning my little house as I thought about this, my sweet, lovely little house. I sang to it. I found that I sung quite a bit. I have a dreadful, tuneless voice, yet I enjoy the sensation of filling my lungs with air and letting out exuberant feelings.

★

My days are joyful. After a peaceful breakfast with Radio 4 for company, I drive to work. I can feel the excitement growing as I get closer to the studio. I don't know what I would do without my students. I love all the chatter and laughter. It is such a great way to start the day. It is August 1981. As I prepare for class the studio is quiet. I hardly have any students, which is normal for this time of year as everyone is away on holiday. But still, even the small classes lift my day and give it structure, purpose. Gently I am trying to find how to live a normal life. I am trying not to take my sleeping pills until bedtime. I am trying not to binge and then throw up. I am finding it so hard. My body has lost the ability to give me correct messages of hunger, of fullness. I get mixed up signals that tell me that I can't be satisfied until I have binged. I try to overcome this but don't always succeed. I do notice that days can go by without me making myself sick. Encouraged, I congratulate myself, 'Well done, Esther,' I pat myself on the back.

I am not entirely on my own as I struggle with these things. I see mother regularly. I am tied to the M4 as I am tied to her. I make plenty of soup and take it with me for our weekends together. She is still quite weak. Her body is trying to reject her teeth implants. She spends a lot of time at the dentist. Soup is a safe food for her and I make it as nourishing as I can. This visit mother can hardly contain her excitement when I arrive.

"One of the students I trained wants to open a studio in Fulham! We'll drive down and look at it later. It's a bit of a ruin at the moment. My student, Gay, wants to rebuild it so there's a studio on the ground floor, a changing room and showers in the basement and her living quarters upstairs."

I haven't seen mother so lively and enthusiastic for ages. Her eyes are bright as is her smile and she can hardly stop talking.

"You know what would make me really happy?" Mother takes hold of my hands. Her warm hands clasp mine in a firm grip, her face comes closer to mine. Her big dark eyes take on an intent stare. It feels like her eyes can penetrate me.

"If you wanted to, you could make me the happiest woman in the world." My heart is beating faster. She looks so serious. Whatever was she going to ask of me now?

"I want you to run the studio, to be the manager, to run classes, to live in London. Oh darling, you could have such a good life and you'd make a lot more money than you do now."

I was stunned. In the silence that followed I had an image of me running this smart studio and always under the eagle eye of my mother. I would never be as perfect as she wanted me to be. Just now my life was on the very brink of becoming the life that I had always wanted after all those years of living the way others wanted me to. I could hear a scream in my head. I heard the voice of that psychiatrist advising me to never live close to my mother or she would eat me up. How quiet the room was as mother waited for my response, still holding onto to me. I looked down at our clasped hands, unable to keep eye contact with her. Her eyes were so dark, so determined to make me answer. I knew the answer I wanted to say straight away, but I knew I wanted to say it in a way that wouldn't make her feel rejected. My mind did briefly skate over her idea. It was true that I would make so much more money. But would I want to live in Fulham or, worse still, in the same block of flats with mother on the 3rd floor, father on the 7th and Aunt Hilde on the 5th? I shuddered to think of it. I would be back in hospital in no time.

"What a fantastic offer," I raised my eyes, smiling at mother. "It's a tough decision. To be honest, I don't think that I could bear to leave my little studio, my lovely students. And I have grown to love living in the country. It would mean leaving friendships. I don't think I am a city girl anymore, I would feel lonely. I'm sorry, mother, I can't give up all that I have worked so hard to build up for myself."

Later I could see what good sense it was for mother to think of having me in one of her studios. She would not feel so competitive with me as she did with other students who went on to teach and she would feel that she was in total control. Mother showed little emotion at my response and we didn't discuss it again for the rest of our visit. I should have known that she was brewing up a response. She was giving herself enough time to work out how best to hit me back. Days later, it came.

"I'm glad I know where you stand now," she spoke calmly without any sign in her voice that she was upset. I could barely perceive a hint of tightness when she spoke but it was so slight, perhaps I imagined it. "I am going to give my Manchester Street studio to Lois. I have also made an appointment with my solicitor. I am changing my will. Everything will go to Lois."

Lois certainly deserved the studio. She had worked for my mother for years. She was the model featured in my mother's book and would soon be the model in the video that was in the pipeline. Lois had always been the most loyal person to mother. She took Lotte's silly behaviour as utter nonsense and took no notice, patting her on the head and saying, 'Yes, boss.' There isn't another person who knew how to handle mother in such a delightful way. Certainly mother would have shot anyone else who treated her in such a manner. Somehow it worked between her and Lois. Mother never took offence and Lois never felt hurt when she was given a going over by the 'Lotte treatment'. Mother appreciated Lois and had even given her a well-deserved bonus in the shape of the deposit on her first house. This house was a dream come true for Lois. I am more than happy for her to take over the studio. It is the right thing for mother to do. Lois and I always got on. Looks of understanding would pass between us in the studio. Lois knew how difficult mother could be and wisely kept her thoughts to herself when she made comments about me.

Back in Hungerford, despite the blow from mother, I am happy. As I walk briskly into the health club, I am looking forward to another session of class. Every week I meet different and, mostly, interesting people. As I pass reception a pretty girl with long blond hair calls me over. In her hand, between her long, red painted fingernails, is an envelope.

"Esther, I've got a letter for you. Look, I'm really sorry, but this came about three weeks ago and I keep missing you or forgetting to put it out."

I take it and look at the handwritten envelope. I don't recognise it. Who could be writing to me here? How odd. It is a puzzle. I can't wait to open it. When I do I start to read: 'Dear Esther, I loved our interesting chat …'

As I have not had an interesting chat for ages I think someone must be having a joke with me. I have chatted with my very nice neighbour but it was never very interesting. Anyway, why would my neighbour be sending me letters here? At first I do not make much sense of what is written, possibly due to rising excitement. The letter continues: 'I'll be passing Hungerford as I take my boat down to Devon to sail. I would love to take you out for tea so we could continue our interesting conversation. Phone me if that is ok.'

This must be a joke. I do not know anyone who has a boat. Eventually I make out the signature and slowly a glimmer starts to glow in the darkness of my memory. Of course! It is that man who was with Miss Sulky at that party. How clever of him to find out the health club address. That was the only thing about me that he had to go on.

I look at the letter again and sigh with relief. The day he was arranging for hasn't passed, but it nearly did. It was on Friday, in only two days. Perhaps he thinks that I do not want to have tea with him and that is why I haven't phoned. How awful. I dial his number as soon as I get home after class. It's engaged. I try again. Still engaged. I can't believe it. I try for over an hour but I won't give up. At last he answers. I apologise and explain the delay in my reply. It's obvious that we are both shy and we giggle a lot. We arrange a time. I'll have to take an extra sleeping pill tonight to get to sleep with all this excitement. I want to shout at the top of my lungs and tell the world that I've got a date! By lunchtime on Friday I am ready. I check in the mirror. Not too much makeup. I don't want to scare him. I am wearing a new dress that mother bought me on our last shopping spree. It is pale turquoise and feels slinky and silky on my body. I run my hands down it and feel a sensuous anticipation. I want to be desired. I have forgotten how that feels. I long to have my sensual side reawakened. I find it hard to imagine what it will feel like to go out with a man after 28 years of marriage during which we rarely went out due to our poverty. What is the etiquette now? A woman's role has changed so much since I last went out on a date. A woman was not expected to pay for herself back then. How about now? Do I offer to pay half? I become hot with discomfort. My ignorance embarrasses me.

I look at the clock and my heart races with excitement. Two o'clock then three o'clock ... What time do people mean when they say teatime? The phone rings. I know that it will be him and it is. He explains that he is still in London and that business has held him up. Would I accept an invitation for dinner instead? He can pick me up at six. Dinner sounds so much more intimate than tea.

"Yes, dinner would be lovely. I'll see you at six," I reply jauntily.

The day is turning out to be one of waiting. I can't settle down enough to do anything. I can't concentrate enough to even read a book. I look in the mirror. My makeup is beginning to look as though it has been on my face too long, which it has. I remove it and put fresh eyeliner, mascara and lipstick. That's better. I scrutinize my face in the mirror. I smile into my reflection. I try a flirting expression and burst out laughing. It looks ridiculous. I'll just stick with the smile. I glance at my watch. It is only five o'clock. He must be on his way now. But he isn't. The phone rings.

"I've been held up but will be with you at seven." He sounds flustered and a bit breathless.

So he should. All day I have been waiting. Perhaps I can understand Miss Sulky's complaining voice after all. Does he do this to other women? It dawns on me that he is a total stranger and that I know nothing about him except that he has a boat, and sails. Oh yes, and he's got a nice smile and blue eyes. That's not much to go on.

My excitement is slightly dampened and a touch of anxiety flutters in my stomach. Thank goodness mother knows about him and a couple of girlfriends know about my date. If they don't hear from me tomorrow they will report me as missing. There will be a police search. They will find my body in a ditch and I'll have been ... oh I can't bear thinking about it. I have talked myself into a dark place. Come on, lighten up a bit, you're going to have a great evening. He will be the perfect gentleman.

It's almost seven now and he hasn't rung again. That must mean that he is on his way. I wonder how he will park a car and a boat outside my house. Living on the High Street, as I do, parking is often a problem. I can't bear the wait any longer. I take a pair of scissors and open the front door and step into the whitewashed passage that leads to the street entrance. There is ivy growing around this external door and trimming it will keep me occupied. As I cut the ivy back in the pretence of busy-ness I keep my eye on the traffic. Unexpectedly there I hear a voice close up behind me.

"Hello."

I leap out of my skin. How did he do that? He is here but where is the boat? How did he slip past my vigilant eyes? I am completely flustered. As I usher him through my front door we face each other, almost touching in this narrow passage that hardly leaves any space for a proper greeting. He quickly brushes my cheek and repeats, 'Hello.'

A rush of blood shoots through my veins. This is chemistry, pure, hot and lustful. I'm shocked by such powerful feelings. I rein it in, pulling myself together.

His boat is parked at the local garage. We go off in his car to the Dundas Arms in Kintbury. When we arrive we sit in a cosy corner for a drink before going into the restaurant for dinner.

"What would you like to drink?"

I shrink inside. I have no idea what to answer. What do people drink when they are on a date? I have kept a safe distance from alcohol. Living with John has taught me its dangers. I do so want a drink, need a drink, hoping it will relax me.

"Gin and tonic," I reply, remembering that in the last play I saw on television that was what they were drinking.

As we sip our drinks we become more comfortable with each other. He turns out to be very sporty, a fresh air kind of person. He does a lot of sailing, cycling, swimming, and walking, so unlike me. What a contrast he is to everyone I have known. My interests lie solely in the arts. I have only ever really known painters, poets, sculptors, actors, dancers. That is my world. How different it is in his. Our experiences don't match up, we have absolutely nothing in common. Nevertheless, by the time we have a finished the bottle of wine that accompanied dinner, I am feeling on top of the world. We may not have much in common but we chat the night away, enjoying each other's company. He holds my hand in the car and all the way home, changing gears in a very unorthodox manner. I love it. What fun. He parks in front of my house, takes me in his arms and kisses me. I feel so dizzy. Is it the drink or the chemistry between us? It is a lethal mixture.

"Come to Devon with me, I'll take you sailing. Say yes. We'll have such a great time," he promises.

"I can't do that. I don't know you," I sound like a child refusing a lift.

"Gamble. Go on, take a gamble."

This felt like a challenge, and right now I was up for any challenge thrown at me. "Okay, I'll come." I don't know if I even knew what I was saying. I leant over towards him to kiss his cheek, "Thank you for a lovely evening." I put my hand on the car door to get out. "Good night," I smiled.

"Hold on, if you are coming with me in the morning then I am going to have to come in and stay the night."

My hand flew up to my mouth. Oh, how stupid could I be, of course he has to stay the night! I giggle at my own stupidity and we both go inside.

"Coffee?" I ask.

"Thank you, yes."

I put the kettle on but never heard it boil.

At five am neither of us had slept at all.

"Time to go," he says, "Pack your swimming costume and we're off."

I yawned all the way to Devon. Sex in a single bed had left no space for sleep. When we got there he checked us into a hotel as man and wife. I stood back feeling awkward and shy. As he signed in, the morning sun streaked across the reception desk and lit up his face. I felt as if I was in a drugged state, as sometimes happens when deprived of sleep, and yet alert, with adrenalin coursing through my veins in a mixture of fear and exhilaration. I bet mother never felt like this on morphine.

"I'd like to phone my mother," I said in a whisper. "She'll be worried if she doesn't hear from me, especially as it's a Bank Holiday. She'll expect me to be in."

He dialled the number I gave him, on the reception desk phone.

"Mother, I'm in Devon with a man," I blurted out, all subtlety lost in my exhaustion. I rattled on at a high speed, more gibberish tumbling out. She asked to speak to this man.

I handed the phone over. He introduced himself, promising her that he wasn't an axe murderer and that he would take the greatest care of me.

"I think your daughter is a very special person, and so beautiful. You must be so proud of her. Please believe me when I say that I will do everything that I can to make this a happy time," he put the phone away from his ear so that I could listen in on what mother was saying.

"Well, I suppose I should be pleased but I do not want you to rob me of my daughter. I've just gotten her back. We had such fun when she was a teenager and I was looking forward to having fun with her again. You are not to take her from me."

A few polite words passed between them after this and then he passed the phone back to me. Mother continued:

"I want you to have fun and enjoy life. It's been good having you back in my life. I just don't want you to settle with a man so soon. By the way, I have nicknamed him Jampot."

I reassured mother that I would always be there for our outings to restaurants, galleries, hotels and other nice places and that that wouldn't change.

"What do you mean you've nicknamed him Jampot?" I asked.

"Well, his initials are JM so that spells jam in my head and jam has to have a pot. Bye darling."

I shouldn't be surprised at how her brain works yet I always find it intriguing. The name Jampot stuck. He will always be my Jampot.

I got such a kick going out to sea in his catamaran, sipping cocktails in the club bar while watching him windsurf, finding lovely old country pubs for meals. As I experienced this new kind of life my bulimic desire to throw up diminished, although at first I felt more out of control and only chose meals that felt safe to keep down. Jampot would drive miles and miles to find an empty beach, a cliff top to walk, a village tearoom, and always holding my hand while driving. I saw more of England than I had ever seen before. Jampot, only three years older than me and already retired, saw life as a holiday.

Of course, I had to keep returning to my studio, but I was not tied down by it. The classes could keep running without me for a while as I had such willing helpers. I took advantage of their kindness and enjoyed the constant outings.

In early September 1981 we were off again for a four-day holiday, this time to Wales. The sun shone every day. The beaches were the best I had ever seen. Didn't anyone know of these great Welsh beaches? Where was everybody? There were just a few stragglers, children with buckets and spades enjoying the last few days of holiday. It was as if everyone who came here knew they had to keep it secret.

I phoned mother regularly knowing how she might be feeling, making sure that she could have a laugh with me and enjoy my happiness instead of feeling left out.

"He's dying to meet you, mother. We'll come to London next weekend. We'll stay in a hotel. Would you rather we came to the flat for a meal or shall we go out?"

Mother's voice has a slight edge to it:

"I hope that you won't end up being hurt. What do you know about this man? I've done lots of things in my life but I have never gone off with a total stranger. I think you are mad."

Nothing will dampen the happiness I feel. I reassure her that so far he has been generous and kind, a real gentleman.

"We constantly chat, he laughs a lot and the sex just gets better and better and there is plenty of it. I'm sure you have experienced men with exceptional stamina."

"Yes, you know I have. I had to ply him with a lot of whisky first but then he could go on forever." We both laugh loudly. I can sense that she is enjoying sharing my adventure and I enjoy telling her about it.

The next time I spend a weekend with her we are on a high.

"How long," I ask mother, "does this euphoria last?"

"Not long, with me it's three months if I'm lucky or haven't destroyed him by then."

"We're still at that stage where we're showing each other our good side. He is my dream man." For a second I feel myself slip into the memory of last night, the heat and excitement. "I suppose we still have a lot to learn about each other. You know, when we are not together he phones me every night. I feel so wanted, so loved. I feel I could become addicted to him."

"Not as dangerous as morphine," mother smiles wryly.

Jampot was a kind, polite, thoughtful man of constant affection. I saw nothing to give me doubt, suspected nothing. I felt like a purring cat, rolling over onto my back, trusting to be loved. Little did I know what was to follow.

*

It was late September when mother phoned one evening, very excited:

"Can you come and stay next weekend?" It sounded almost like a command rather than a question.

Mother loved being secretive and a little mischievous so I had no idea what lay ahead. It all spilled out within seconds of my arrival. She was bursting with excitement.

"Vidal Sassoon wants to meet me for a chat. Well, I don't think it is just a chat. Something serious is going on. I don't want to go on my own. I want you to be there with me when we talk."

Now I was the one who was excited:

"Of course, mother. How terrific! I can't wait."

"He has asked me to come round to the hotel where he and Beverley are staying, at about six. Maybe that is where they want to have drinks before they go out to eat."

I tried to visualise the scene. I saw myself as though I was in a film: smart hotel, beautiful people. I couldn't believe how much my life had changed since I left John.

We arrived by taxi. Mother had lent me one of her designer trouser suits. We looked good. We were shown into Vidal Sassoon's suite. He opened the door, expecting us. The first thing that struck me was his skin. It had a smoothness about it that had an almost translucent quality, so polished and cared for. His smile was warm and welcoming. Beverley came in from the bedroom. She was truly stunning. Every hair on her head was perfectly styled. She was flawless. Her skin radiated youth and health. She was beautiful. They looked like a dream couple, the American dream, and I was thrilled to be so close. After he offered us drinks we got down to business. As we sipped freshly pressed orange juice I listened carefully to all that Vidal had to say. Was he really saying what I thought he was saying? I could hardly breathe for listening. Mother sat silently, not even nodding her head. Occasionally she sipped her juice. She had no expression on her face, no hint of a smile, just listening intently.

Then the meeting was over and we headed out to mother's favourite Indian restaurant. Once we sat down she relaxed and looked at the menu.

"I don't know why I bother, I know exactly what I want anyway."

She nodded towards the waiter.

"For goodness sake, mother, tell me what you are thinking!"

I had been bowled over by Vidal Sassoon's suggestion that he would like to discuss, in proper business terms and with a solicitor, the opening of Lotte Berk studios in his salons. Well, mother could then have even more of everything she loved: money, fame, status. Although I was starving, I was used to eating dinner closer to six pm than this; my stomach felt so knotted that I could hardly swallow anything. Mother, on the other hand, was fuelled by the food and began to rant.

"I know what he is after," the words spat out of mother's mouth (thankfully her teeth were cemented well into place). "He wants to use my name."

At that I nearly collapsed. Vidal Sassoon wanting to use mother's name! Was she serious? One look into her eyes and I knew she was.

"He just wants to make money out of me like everyone does."

If he was going to make money out of her, how much more money was she going to make collaborating with him? I could hardly believe that she was in her right mind.

"Everyone is out to do me. I can't and won't trust anyone, especially after what happened with that American girl in New York. All that charm. He can schmooze me as much as he wants. I'm not falling for all that talk. I've learnt my lesson."

The American experience she spoke of, the one that had left her, a natural paranoiac, even more paranoid, had happened in the early 1970s. A most attractive blond woman, Lydia Bach, had approached mother saying she wanted to train in her method and open a studio in New York. Mother was dazzled by her attention and constant flattery, as well as finding her American brashness amusing. At the end of the training she handed mother a large amount of money, in cash. Mother's eyes drank in the sight of so many banknotes and she signed the contract without having it vetted by a lawyer. Mother had signed away all the American and Canadian rights for her exercises. Lydia opened a huge studio in Manhattan, as well as one in Los Angeles, and all for the sum of $7,000 a year until mother's death. Later, when mother realized what she had done and wanted to change this contract, lawyers couldn't break it. What really hurt mother was having to turn down offers for books and videos from the States. All that fame could have been hers, though at least her name was still attached to Lydia's studios.

Seventeen

An exercise from my first book.
Mother told me not to smile.

Snow was falling like fine powder. My garden had little foot-prints on it where birds had searched for food. Although delightful to look at, the treacherous weather had locked us in. I wasn't really keen to go outside my little house. The ugly gas fire gave out quite a good heat. I lay curled up in Jampot's arms feeling our own warmth. This housebound weekend was punctuated by eating what we could find in the fridge, and sex. And then some more sex. This was a wonderful way to keep warm. The weather stayed bad for two days and I could-n't get to work. I hadn't expected to so enjoy being snowed in.

Jampot and I began to exchange histories. We were getting to know each other, yet I couldn't make him out. There was something strange about him. As much as I dug and delved into his psyche I found I understood him less and less. We lay naked together and suddenly he gave me a big squeeze:

"Let's go away. You would enjoy a holiday, wouldn't you? People who can't enjoy holidays can't enjoy life."

What an odd statement to make. Of course I agreed. I mentioned how lovely the Spanish villa that mother had taken me to had been. It was not only lovely but also only a short drive from Marbella and a few steps from the beach. Perfect. We asked mother if we could rent this villa from her friend and then bought the plane tickets.

Before we knew it we were snuggled up to each other as the thrust of the plane soared us towards another adventure. We were going to be away together for two whole weeks. If my excitement could turn me into a shower of colours I would be a walking rainbow.

When we arrived we had no problems finding the villa or the hired car. As we drove to the villa we were met with a surprise. Once secluded and nestled amongst trees and bushes, cleverly designed not to overlook anyone else, the villa now had a huge Hilton Hotel towering over it. It was not such an exclusive little place anymore.

Despite the inauspicious start we were determined to enjoy this escape together. At first I didn't notice the slight oddness in Jampot's behaviour. Every morning began in the same way.

"Come on Esther, get up. Let's go."

"Where?" I had not realised there was a routine or a plan.

"Shopping, we need to go to the supermarket. We need to stock up more."

"We did that yesterday."

"Well, we are going to have to go again today."

"You go, I'll meet you down at the beach."

This seemed a logical suggestion, as all he would be stocking up on was bread and oranges. The fridge was still full of good, wholesome salad foods that I would throw together for our lunch. Evening meals were usually eaten out, so there was not really any need to go shopping. Was he obsessed with bread and oranges? Jampot came up close to me. His broad shoulders, which had always made me feel safe and secure, now felt menacing. He placed a hand on my shoulder. Although the pressure was light I felt paralysed. His eyes looked cold and unblinking.

"If you had any real feelings, if you loved me, you would want to be with me at all times. When I go shopping I want you with me."

I thought, but knew better than to say, how ridiculous he was being. His tone of voice let me know that this was no joke. For the rest of the holiday we went shopping every morning together. After our shopping trip we sat on the beach together enjoying the warm sunshine. It was only April and England was still covered in snow. This felt like such a gift. This gift was slightly spoiled when I looked over at Jampot. 'What an extraordinary way to eat oranges,' I thought to myself, not daring to mention it. He ripped the top end of the peel off with his teeth and then sucked out the centre flesh of the orange. The slurping noise that accompanied this was disgusting. I kept my eyes averted.

"Does me eating oranges like this put you off?" Jampot stared at me.

"No, no," I replied with an instinct of self-protection.

The sea was still a bit cold for me to swim in but hardy Jampot was in and out of the water frequently. He filled up with oranges in between dips. It was either oranges or loaves of bread that he would tear and eat in handfuls. This was why we had to do our morning shopping ritual every day.

"I do have a bit of an eating problem," he confessed to me one evening over a bottle of wine and a loaf of bread. "I'm a binge eater. So as to not get fat I keep my binging down to only oranges and bread."

I didn't mention that I also had an eating problem that I was battling with. I thought that I was conquering it but some-how Jampot's binging made me feel that I had permission to indulge in my own.

As the holiday continued I felt that Jampot was changing. He was not as relaxed, not as easygoing. He never let me out of his sight. Even when I was in the bath he insisted on the bathroom door being left open. I started to notice him look-ing through the crack in the door as I bathed. I sang nursery rhymes to myself, partly to comfort myself and partly so he would not know how rattled I felt when he watched me.

I managed short moments of escape from his constant pres-ence by insisting that I had a siesta. I was curled up on my bed one afternoon and had the spooky feeling of being watched. I rolled over and there stood Jampot, on the other side of the picture window, his face close as he watched me from the gar-den. He was just standing and staring at me.

I was now in a constant state of alertness. I knew that this man was mad. I had to keep him in a state of trust. I did all that was asked of me. This was not like walking on eggshells, this was like walking on sharp needles. I had to take great care. There were days when I thought that perhaps it was me that was mad. I was tense and afraid all the time and felt so far away from home. And then a migraine came from out of the blue. I never really suffered from them. The pain was horrendous and seeped into every part of my body. I dared not move. I could not even be touched. Every so often the pain shot through me. I lay on the bed willing my headache to go. Jampot was patient but only up to a point. He paced the villa sucking oranges at intervals. He walked in silence. I could never hear him enter the bedroom but I sensed it and would open my eyes to see him standing over me.

"Better yet?" he inquired, smiling.

"No, the pain is tearing my head apart."

Not so surprising, I thought, as I am so tense, so frightened. I might as well have been standing on a cliff's edge waiting to be pushed over. I had never experienced so much fear. What was happening? Who had he turned into and what would happen next?

"What you need is some fresh air." A smile was on his face as he said this. I noticed that it didn't reach his eyes. "I always feel better after a brisk walk."

'I bet you do,' I thought. 'I also bet you have never had a real migraine before. You have no idea what I am feeling.' It was obvious that he wanted to go for a walk but not on his own. I no longer trusted him. My constant thought was, 'What's your game?' What was he going to do next to scare me to death, to give him power over me? I was coming to the conclusion that he used fear as a control and played mind games to confuse me so that he always had power.

From my past I had learned how to handle a man with a drink problem. I had learned how to understand the moods of the creative mind. I had learned how to handle poverty and hardship. But to me, this new thing was incomprehensible and I was totally unprepared for it. This was a mind so unpredictable that I didn't know what would come next.

By now it was late afternoon and Jampot had become restless. There was an underlying anxiety that I sensed might turn into panic and a loss of control. He certainly couldn't handle losing control. How was I to protect myself? How was I to survive my terror and confront the situation? I decided that my best plan was to go along with everything that Jampot wanted. I had to fall back on everything I learned in drama school and be utterly convincing. He frequently had remarked how good he felt when I was happy. That would be my game.

Now I would do all I could to appear happy and carefree so that he didn't pick up on my mounting fear.

"Okay, I really do feel bad but I'll try a walk. Perhaps you are right after all."

As I gently got up from the bed the pain was blinding. I tried to think of all the agony and torture my family must have suffered under the Nazis. I was lucky I only had a headache and two weeks with a madman. I would be home soon. I still had my own life.

He put on his swimming trunks and we strolled along the beach. The sea was calm. The sun started to set. Most people had gone home, there was just the occasional couple walking by hand in hand. We also walked holding hands. My steps were slow as each one shot pain through my head.

"I'm just going in for a dip," Jampot kissed my brow before running into the sea and disappearing under the water.

The beach was now deserted. I gently took a few steps, glad to be on my own for a few minutes. I looked out to sea, checking how far out he had got. Jampot frequently went to his local swimming pool and was a very strong swimmer. If I was with him when he went to the pool I would sit on the side amongst the proud parents who were watching their children's progress. Even though the air in the swimming pool was warm and wet and breathing it wasn't very nice, these jaunts to the swimming baths were necessary. Jampot had to have some form of exercise every day. He had explained to me that if he was deprived of a daily run, swim or cycle ride it would mess with his head. I should have heard alarm bells then. It took this holiday to find out how much these neuroses were a part of his life.

My eyes scanned the sea. He wasn't visible. He had only been in for a few minutes, he couldn't have got that far out to sea. I stared and I stared. But there was nothing, no sign of him. What was he up to? He couldn't be swimming underwater for all of this time. The beach was empty and, as far as I could see, so was the Med, right up to the horizon. I felt too ill to hang about and play whatever game he had in mind. I decided that I would make my way back to our villa and go back to bed. As I walked I kept looking back out to sea and along the beach for signs of him. It was as though he had never existed. Was I going mad? I couldn't think straight with the pain throbbing in my head. I heard nothing. There was no crunch on the sand, no sounds of breathlessness. Then from nowhere I was tapped on my shoulder. I screamed and shot round but, of course, he wasn't on the side of the shoulder that he had touched. He was on the other side of me, grinning, amused at how clever he had been to scare me. With my heart now thumping and my head about to burst I lost control.

I yelled at him: "You idiot! You stupid idiot! Are you mad?"

At last I climbed into bed and pulled the covers up to my chin. All I wanted was to keep very still, to never move again.

"Can I get you something?" Jampot had become a little kinder. This may be because he had been shocked at my outburst, or maybe it was dawning on him that I truly was in pain.

"I would love a weak black coffee, please."

As he walked out of the room he forgot to turn the light off. It was not quite dark outside but inside it was. The light hurt my eyes.

I called out:

"Jampot, could you please turn out the light?"

The effort of calling out shot more pain through my head. I yelled again, louder. I know he must have heard me. He didn't come so I crawled out of bed and turned the light off myself. A few minutes later he returned with my coffee and put the light on. I sipped the warm liquid gratefully and then spat it out with an, 'Ugh!'

"This isn't my coffee. This is your decaffeinated stuff that you know I hate."

Jampot only drank decaf and I always had my own jar of coffee because I couldn't stand his.

"I'm sorry," he hung his head. "But I think you should drink decaffeinated while you have such a bad headache."

"I can't drink it. Please make me the weak black coffee that I asked for."

He disappeared once more, leaving the light on again. I didn't bother to shout. I just waited for my warm drink. I wanted it so badly. Jampot came back in with my coffee. Again I sipped it. Again I spat it out.

"What are you doing to me? All I want is a cup of coffee. This is decaffeinated again!"

"Yes," he replied sheepishly. "I didn't think that you could tell the difference and I wanted to prove it to you."

At this point I knew I had to get away. But how? We still had one week to go. I did not think that I could hold out for that long with this madman. The following day I suggested that he went out without me whilst I recuperated quietly in the garden. I played happy with much smiling, hoping that he would soon forget my outburst about the coffee. My instinct warned me to be gentle with him and to let him believe that all was well again. I was becoming extremely concerned for my welfare. I had already noticed that when Jampot became anxious or felt criticized his head turned into a jumbled mess of thoughts that he found overwhelming. The only way he had learnt to sort them out was to exercise. After going for a run or a vigorous swim he would appear fairly normal again. I decided that the best plan was for me to dash across to the

Hilton Hotel and phone mother the next time he went off to exercise. It was possible that she would be able to buy a plane ticket and send it to me so that I could return home sooner. I did not have a penny with me; Jampot had insisted that I brought no money with me on the holiday. He wanted it to be his treat. At the time I was touched by his generosity. Now I felt that his kindness had imprisoned me.

I put on a casual voice, not wishing to arouse any suspicion:

"Sweetheart, could you lend me a fiver? I thought that I might phone mother and let her know what a great time we are having."

Clearly this worked as he handed me a five-pound note and off he went, happy to be getting some exercise. He had the look of a schoolboy let out early, his firm, brown legs sprinting down the road that led to the beach.

I didn't know how much time I had. I needed to speak to my mother well out of his hearing. As soon as he was out of sight I made my way to the hotel. As a shortcut I scrambled through the very thick hedge of the villa garden. My skimpy tee shirt was no armour against the sharp twigs that tore at me. I pushed through the dense foliage with determination and soon appeared in the grounds of the Hilton a dishevelled mess. I walked briskly past the sun worshippers on their loungers. As I entered the hotel lobby where the phones were I sighed with relief at achieving this minor escape. I handed over my money and gave mother's phone number to the man behind the desk who was attending the phones. Glancing in a mirror as I waited, I noticed that my hair had bits of leaves in it and I looked very much in need of some loving care. After a few moments the chap explained in his very thick accent that all lines to England were busy and that I must wait. Oh lord, how long do I dare to wait? If Jampot returned and found me not in he would come here looking for me. I didn't have much time. They tried the lines again. No, all lines to England are still engaged. I decided that it was too dangerous to stay away any longer and asked for my fiver back. I returned to the villa discouraged, although not as dishevelled as I used the conventional route instead of the bushes. I had only just sat down on my lounger when Jampot appeared breathless and grinning. He had obviously unrattled himself. I returned the fiver, knowing that now I had to stay and see the holiday through to the end. My acting skills became my most important asset and invaluable in my survival.

I promised myself that the second we arrived in England I was most definitely finishing with Jampot.

Eighteen

Mother, in exercise.

Mother loved the account of my Spanish escapade. She laughed riotously, throwing her head back and wanting to hear it again and again. Each time I retold it she roared as if it was the first time she had heard it. Despite being mildly concerned that it all could have gone badly wrong, it was too amusing a tale for her to dwell long on the darker side. Repeating these events to her was the best therapy I could have had. All that angst, it was quite ridiculous. I was starting to find it amusing myself.

Life back in Hungerford seemed a touch quiet. There were no phone calls and nothing much happening. Classes were fine. Coffee with the girls was fine. But something was missing. I had not realised what a chunk of life Jampot had injected into my world. What did I really miss? The abundance of affection he gave me. Being made to feel special. Being put on a pedestal. Being adored. Being treated to lovely outings. Great sex. It's not a bad list. I had never been given so much attention, never been so valued and appreciated when I was a child or as a wife. And now I missed it. So what if he is obsessive about cleanliness? John had not been meticulous about his hygiene, far from it. It had been a joy to smell Jampot. It had even been amusing that he didn't like my feet to get dirty on slushy kerbside gutters. He would pick me up and hold me under his arm like a sack of potatoes, his other hand full of shopping, and stride across the road. I found that hilarious. And then there was the time I questioned him about my fridge door. He always washed his hands after touching it.

"Is my fridge so dirty?" I asked.

"No, no, it is just me. Of course your fridge door isn't dirty. It's just a habit, take no notice."

On the other hand, going up an escalator with Jampot was less of a joke. If I rested my hand on the handrail he would slap it off, 'Don't touch that. You don't know how many filthy hands have been on there before you.'

Weighing up the two sides of Jampot became an interesting pastime. I had always been fascinated by the workings of the mind. A few years earlier I had helped out in a psychiatric hospital for a year as an occupational therapist. Remembering how utterly bizarre and irrational many of the patients were calmed my anxieties about Jampot, gave me perspective. He wasn't mad. Maybe I had just exaggerated his oddities. It was all such a new experience for me, being in a relationship with someone new. And so I talked myself into believing he was just a little strange, nothing more.

Jampot started to phone again. No pressure to meet, he just wanted to talk. He was once again the Jampot I had first met, enjoying a chat, warm and complimentary. The calls became more frequent.

"What shall I do, mother?' I asked one day as we sat in the Churchill Hotel, mother's favourite, lingering over a smoked salmon lunch. "You have no idea how much I miss him."

Mother's dark eyes looked into my soul. She gave me her full attention:

"Sex is such a powerful draw. You also have such fun with

him, and what's more, you make me laugh when you tell me about what he does. Would it be so bad to put up with some of his crazy ways when you have someone who loves you so much?"

Often mother would say just what I wanted to hear with matters of the heart. I drove home that Sunday feeling spring in my heart. After all, it was May, that merry month. That evening when Jampot phoned he asked the question I so wanted to hear.

"Yes it would be lovely to meet up," I purred down the phone.

He suggested that we meet in London and he would book a nice place for lunch. This was perfect, no ties, no pressure, just lunch. It felt exciting, romantic and full of promise.

I stayed in London with mother the night before our date. She was in her element, fussing around me before I left, making sure that I looked absolutely marvellous. This was mother at her best, full of fun and mischief, revelling in the situation.

The restaurant was posh and obviously very expensive. If I hadn't been so excited I might have felt intimidated. I almost lost my breath seeing him again. We flirted, we lingered, we touched hands. I completely forgot the Spanish holiday Jampot who had so terrified me. This was the Jampot I had first fallen for. And I was falling again. How could someone be two so very different people? I realised that if I was going to make this work I would have to learn how to deal with these two personalities and find a way to enjoy the good and ignore the bizarre. And so the roller coaster started again. Jampot wooed me. I didn't resist. Soon we were lovers again. I found that when Jampot explained some of his little eccentricities such as his constant need to wash his hands it was easier to cope with it. He told me thought he might have a leaning towards OCD (obsessive compulsive disorder).

"I've got it under control." he reassured me. "Don't give it a second thought; it really is only a mild form of OCD."

Later I read up on the condition, which helped me to understand him and his odd ways a bit more. It also helped me be more tolerant.

Weekends were fun and exciting again. Sometimes we stayed in London and, after spending some time with mother, we would go to the theatre. Other weekends we might go to Wales or Devon, Yorkshire or Norfolk. In between these jaunts I managed to have some weekends with mother on my own, regaling her with stories of our time together.

Meanwhile Gay's Fulham studio was near completion. It was going to be fabulous. Mother still hadn't completely forgiven me for not taking up her offer of running the studio but I had gained strength from my decision to stay in Hungerford. I was ready to put down roots. My own studio was so important to me; my students had become my family. I had too much that I valued in my own life to be persuaded to give it up for the temptations of a London studio. And to top it all off, I was secretly so thrilled to be back with Jampot, despite my friends giving me a hard time.

"What do you think you are doing letting that madman back in your life?" they would ask.

I couldn't admit how much I needed his lovingness, his affection. I loved feeling wanted and so appreciated. This had such a huge affect on my journey of healing. Jampot helped me in other ways, too, although he never realised it. His eating problems highlighted to me that I had not properly dealt with my own. The more repulsed I became watching him suck his oranges, the more I was confronted by my own eating disorder. The suck and slurp of this ritual of his was disgusting but no more disgusting than me putting my finger down my throat. I had to stop. It would be more useful if I concentrated on my own eating problems rather than being repulsed by his.

Jampot never knew about my secret problem. This helped me to work things out for myself. I don't think I could have coped with him asking me after every meal, 'Did you throw it up?' He would not have appreciated paying for something that ended up down the pan.

It didn't take a genius to see how the problem had developed. For so long being passive had made my life easier. My father was always a very passive man. Mother was a different story. I was terrified of her. Her hysterical outbursts paralysed me with fear, even though they were rarely aimed at me. More often they were directed towards her sister, my Aunt Hilde, or my father, or even the cats. Her outbursts exploded out of the blue and could be heard all over the house. Perhaps through fear, I allowed my mother to be in total control of all that I did. Not that I saw that at the time. She always knew best and I believed her when she said that. Once I grew up a bit, what did I go and do next? I married a man who had to be in control at all times. I wasn't allowed to drive for years, not until I started teaching my classes and getting a little independence for myself. On the domestic front I had been given some freedom. I could shop, cook, clean the house. That was acceptable. But other than that I had no say in my life, no power. It did feel like a big joke that once I got free from my mother I put myself in a marriage with a man who needed to have control. And then to divorce him and find myself with a controlling lover!

Eventually the changes that took place in my new life woke me up to these issues. I realised that perhaps my eating disorder was a way to feel like I had control over something. Of course that wasn't quite true. I no longer had control over bulimia. It was beyond that. I now had the hard work of finding a way of mastering what had become over the years a comforting and destructive habit.

I felt like a picture was slowly emerging, revealing the patterns in my life. Things needed to change. 'First things first,' I told myself. I have to tackle my eating problem. Having bulimia had confused my brain. I no longer had the ability to know when I was hungry and only felt satisfied once I had thrown up. When binging I could eat a lot. So much food in my stomach made throwing up easier. I found the answer: I cut down on the amounts that I ate and didn't touch food between meals. When I ate small amounts it was much harder to throw up. My craving to binge fought with my desire to stop this destructive cycle. A huge battle now engulfed me. My desire to eat consumed me. I felt empty in more ways than one now that I was not filling up my neediness with food. More and more I became aware of how starved my life was of meaning. Now and again I would succumb and have a fantastic binge. For a short moment it felt wonderful but this satisfaction then turned to anger and disappointment in myself. The battle continued. Slowly though, the bouts between my healthy self and my sick self became less frequent. It took nearly a year for my body and brain to understand what having an appetite felt like and better still, now I could listen to it. This was the beginning of turning my empty self into a healthy self.

Nineteen

Me in 1999, having a think.

I have been blessed with two of the greatest friends, my sons Michael and Jo. They have been my constant support. They embrace me with their enduring love, warmth, humour and affection. Michael, with his rational brain and solid logic, gives me food for thought and helps keep my feet on the ground. His good sense compliments Jo's philosophical brain, awareness and wisdom. Jo teaches me to think creatively. His unwavering belief in me, his constant compliments and frequent phone calls have helped heal my wounded ego. Both of them have a sense of fun and optimism that gives me joy. At this time, the early 1980s, the boys' support became more important to me as mother and I were once again in a period of cool communication since my refusal to run the Fulham studio. The fun that we used to share had not been with us for a while. I didn't feel like I wanted to amuse her with tales of Jampot's escapades, especially not when she acted as if a smile would crack her face into pieces. Phone calls were polite, trips to London short.

Always unpredictable, one day she began to thaw. I never knew or understood what change had gone on inside her for this to happen. Had father had a word with her? Had friends? Whatever the reason, I was so happy to have her friendship back again. I looked forward to our weekends together now that all was well again. My car flew along the M4 towards London. It only had three cylinders but with the wind behind me I could rattle along at 80 miles per hour. The blossoms of May brought life into spring as I whizzed past. When I arrived we went for a coffee. Then we went on to lunch at a creperie. Mother only had sweet ones with sugar and lemon. I am now the healthy eater and had savoury ones filled with vegetables.

Later that evening we laid down on the bed with a bowl of grapes and cherries between us, vaguely watching television and chatting. She turned the sound down.

"One of my students has been discussing money with me. She suggested that I change my bank to Coutts," she said. "So, I did, last week. I had an appointment with the nicest young man. We talked about so many things. I am very excited by what he was telling me. He is now my personal bank manager."

I was speechless. Mother interested in being sensible about money? That's a new one. Since she started having money all I could see was how much she enjoyed spending it. I was intrigued.

"He wants to put my money into stocks and shares. I don't really understand what that means but I gather it will make money, something called interest."

I had no idea how much money my mother had and she had made it clear to me that she would never tell me. I wondered if she remembered the will she had made. God forbid that I should mention that.

"He talked about property being a sensible investment. I don't see why. In Germany most people rent and I am happy renting. I love my flat and I won't ever move. The only way I will leave here is feet-first."

Something must have been stirring in her brain.

"I can see the sense in you buying a place, though. You're young and you don't know what will happen in the future."

"Yes," I agreed. "I can see the sense in it as well and it would certainly help me feel secure and independent."

"Why don't you see what's on the market that's reasonable, you know, a small, cheap little place. I am prepared to give you the money if it doesn't make too much of a dent in my savings."

To say I was surprised and taken aback doesn't begin to express the thoughts and feelings that flooded through me. Of course I was thrilled. Of course I was excited. But was this one of mother's promises, like the au pair so many years ago, promptly forgotten once I was out of sight? This time at least she wasn't on drugs so perhaps I could believe her. I was not going to let myself doubt her. I threw my arms around her, crushing the grapes as well as her in my embrace. I loved her. I kissed and hugged her, wanting her to feel my joy and gratitude.

"I am making a lot of money now and I am very proud of myself. If only my father was alive to see what I have achieved. I want to do this for you. Just think how wonderful it makes me feel to be able to do this for my daughter."

★

Going around estate agents was a completely new experience for me, as was discussing what kind of house that I want. How many rooms? Is there a garden? How much does it cost? To my own ears I sound rich. I really cannot believe that I am talking like this. This is how I expect others to speak, not me. I do not want my heart to stop beating with joy. I do not want this to stop. I do not want to wake from this perfect dream only to find myself in the damp smelly cottage from my past, with no sunlight and no warmth. My happiness spills through into every hour of my day.

At last I find a sweet cottage-style house down a quiet back street of Hungerford. It is love at first sight. There are two small bedrooms. There is a skylight in the kitchen letting the sun stream in. The garden is neat and tidy. I can see myself sitting in it, sunning myself when the weather warms up. It is perfect. I phone mother. She is excited and tells me to go ahead. £27,000. That sounds like a fortune. Still, she said go ahead. All is well. The estate agent is happy. I am happy. I have no idea what lies ahead, what pitfalls await my ignorance and innocence. I imagine that since I have agreed to buy the house there is nothing to do but wait for the sale to go through, that all is settled.

I get a call from the estate agent a week later. The property has gone up by a thousand pounds. I phone mother. My heart has a certain anxiety beating in it. But no, it is okay.

"Fine," I tell the agent.

Another week goes by. The agent phones again. The owners of what I already see as my cottage have had a better offer: £31,000. I tell mother. As I relay the news over the telephone I can feel that something is up. She is very quiet and when she does speak she hesitates.

"I know how disappointing this will be for you, but that is

just too much money." There is a long pause. The silence conveys more than the words. "I have also been thinking," she continues, her voice sharp like it is accusing me of something. "Perhaps you haven't thought of how I would feel parting with so much money."

I stay silent, unsure of what's coming.

"I can't honestly see why you have to buy a house. What's wrong with renting? I've had some sleepless nights worrying about how I'd feel giving you so much. I know I can afford it but that is not the point. Just the thought of all that money. Parting with so much leaves me feeling vulnerable and insecure. Think of it as my refujew mentality. I'm sorry darling but I simply can't give you any money."

After reassuring mother that I did understand, which of course I did, I came off the phone and burst into floods of tears. These turned into great breathless sobs as I mourned the house that I had let myself believe would be mine.

A few weeks later my father came to visit me with his third, and very young, wife. We sat in our local cafe together, father's sweet tooth getting the better of him as plates of cakes were brought to our table. Where did he put it all? He was still slim and in great shape, even though he was now over 70-years-old. Age hadn't diminished his good looks. I recount the house fiasco to them both. I'm still hurting from it and want to talk about it. Father responds by defending mother. He always did, why didn't I expect it by now? His wife, with an air of authority and a sharp tone that could slice through cream cakes interrupts:

"No one in their right mind would give you a mortgage. Get used to the idea of renting. You will never own your own home."

The experience of house hunting and the dreams that came

with it had made me even more determined to buy my own house. I am taken aback by her certainty that this will never be possible. Then I feel the stubborn child in me rise up. I smile at her and nod my head:

"I expect you're right."

Inside, another voice emerges and silently says, 'I'll show you, I'll prove you are wrong.' I can feel energy and strength returning. With confidence I decide that I will buy my own house and I'll do it on my own. I feel good. House hunting starts again. From anger, stubbornness and the desire to rise to a challenge my ambition was born. I was determined that I would succeed. This became my driving force, despite the great odds I was against.

I restarted my search. After a little while I found a house in Hungerford and within the budget I thought I would be able to manage. Trouble was, it looked ugly, so working-class. Some of mother's snobbishness has rubbed off on me. As I go for a viewing I can hear her voice in my head. I want to tune it out. I want to like this place. I ring the doorbell. A scruffy young woman answers the door carrying a young child astride her hip. Two more children hang around her legs.

"Who is it?" a shrill woman's voice shouts out from somewhere within.

"It's the lady come to see the house."

A dog barks and appears, limping, fat and with a matted coat. I smile, pat the dog and immediately regret it. I smile at the children but they look bored and don't smile back. I am introduced to the grandmother who stays stuck in her chair. Another dog appears. This one is snappy and small. I avoid touching this one. I want to leave. The smell of boiled cabbage and urine cause my throat to constrict.

I can hardly remember what the house had to offer. I

remember how crowded it was, the bright red and gold swirls on the carpet, the dirty children, the husband who suddenly appeared with a half smoked rolly stuck to his lip and wearing what might have once been a white vest. I got into my car and cried and cried. All my excitement dissipated, my dreams felt deflated. I couldn't phone mother and let her know my disappointment but I needed to cry on someone's shoulder. I phoned my good friend Nicky.

"It's awful, horrid, you have no idea," I wailed down the phone.

"Go and look at it again and I'll come with you. I'm sure it can't be that bad," Nicky tried to calm me.

I arranged another viewing. Maybe she was right. Maybe I was just overreacting. We saw the house together. Nicky, the most positive and enthusiastic person I knew, came out of the viewing silent. I've never known her not to speak or voice some opinion. We went to the pub.

"Look," Nicky said in the practical sounding voice she only uses when she wants to sound sensible. "You can't really afford anything better. It's a good price, £25,000. It needs a good clean and a lick of paint and I know it's hard to believe but you will get that horrid smell out. I will help you. I admit, I did get a shock at first but you must look beyond that. It's not perfect. That shouldn't stop you from making it into a lovely home for yourself and your new life. Come on Esther, buck up. I'll get us another drink."

The next morning I planned to see the estate agent. Nicky was right, it was a cheap possibility because of its terrible state. It was sensible to make an offer.

The next day a letter arrives from my cousin. How unusual, he never writes. The letter states that our Aunt Margaret died some months ago. This was not really surprising as she had been an alcoholic since her teens. What surprised us all was that she lived well into her seventies. Even more surprising was the cheque for £2,000 enclosed within the folds of this letter, a little legacy from her to me. What fantastic timing. I had already hidden away the advance from my book and had some tiny savings set aside as well. I planned to use these to get my mortgage and a few pots of paint. My spirits rose again.

The estate agent put in my offer for £23,000. This was accepted and I was sent across the road to a building society to arrange a mortgage. At 49 I know that it will be difficult for me to get a first mortgage, especially with my history and income. Trying to look confident and smart, trying to look like someone who could be a businesswoman, I walk into the building society. My relaxed posture as I sit opposite the young man who can make true or deny all my dreams belies how nervous I am. If I listened to my true feelings I would be down on my knees pleading to him, please, please don't refuse me this mortgage. Instead I stay calm and make sure I make good eye contact with him. He is in his twenties, perhaps early-thirties. Despite his power in this situation I do not feel in the least intimidated by him. I am thankful that he is just a boy in comparison to me since I frequently feel intimidated by men in authority.

I answer his questions and as I do it becomes clear to me that in no way do I fulfil the requirements necessary to be offered a mortgage. My father's wife was right; no one in their right mind would offer me one.

"Where are you working at the moment?" he asks.

"At my local Health Hydro." This is absolutely true; I do two hours a week there. He is delighted. His eyes light up.

"I've just joined. It's a fantastic place. My membership includes swimming, sun bed, massage ... " he rattles on enthusiastically.

I smile and nod encouragingly. He is very impressed by the Health Hydro. It is posh and plush and designed to cater for the rich and famous. For some reason he never asks me what I do there or for how many hours I do it. I wonder if he thinks I run the place. He doesn't probe too deeply about finances. I explain that I only recently started working there after leaving my husband. He is uncomfortable and seems to not want to intrude on what might be an emotional subject for me.

"I am just getting my books straight. I run a private studio as well. It is still early days." I speak in a confident and relaxed way as if I know what I am talking about.

I know that I have enough to put down a deposit on the house. But I also know that I do not have enough income to meet the monthly repayments. This has not occurred to the boy and I stay silent. I know that as soon as I move in I shall advertise for a lodger. Mother has also offered to pay the monthly repayments for one year. I'm nearly home and dry.

The boy relapses into rapture about belonging to such a prestigious health club. What is going on in his head? He finishes the interview, stands up and stretching out his hand to shake mine he says he'll be in touch soon and that it has been a pleasure meeting me. I do believe in angels. My angel has been working miracles. I got the mortgage.

My son Jo, his current girlfriend and Jampot helped me move in. Nicky had been right. It didn't take too long to rid the house of all the stinking carpets and slap on some fresh paint. I never even had to advertise for a lodger. I was having a cup of tea in the very same cafe that my father and his wife had shared cake and disappointment in not so long ago. I asked the proprietor to listen out for anyone who was looking for a room. A week later a young girl came round asking about a room. Wow. Within a few months I was the owner of a house and a landlady. Life certainly had changed. Settling into my new house and new life brought with it a new confidence. I enjoyed the company of my lodger. We exchanged boyfriend stories and giggled. My girlie side surprises me. The last time I felt girlie was in Paris when Red and I would stroll along the streets arm in arm and tell each other everything. My lodger, Rosemary, soon became a great friend.

I am trying to fight my growing irritation with Jampot. The balance of my life feels like it is changing. I am less needy. I still enjoy the affection I get from Jampot and the fabulous sex and the wonderful treats he offers me but I feel less dependent, less infatuated. We escaped together to Paris, had a spell in the South of France and spent another holiday in Normandy. It is hard to let go of this new lifestyle that I share with Jampot yet I cannot deny the fact that the longer we stay together the less I feel for him. I sense a growing conflict within me as I build my own life and feel more confident and rooted. I do not know how long this would have gone on. Fate took the decision out of my hands, as it so often does.

This April was a vicious, cold and stormy month. After a week up north together Jampot and I were driving back home when without warning he pulled the car over on the top of a cliff and parked the car close to the edge. The coastline seemed far away below us. There was not even a rugged path to get down to the sea, just jagged rocks. The sea was deepest, darkest grey. Waves frothed and slammed into each other and the shore. This was the set for a horror film, only it was for real.

"I need to go for a swim," Jampot announced.

With amazing dexterity he changed into his swimming trunks as we sat in the front seat. He was a very strong man, physically tough, but even he had a job getting the car door open. The wind pushed like a stormy temper, hitting the car as Jampot got out. Of course, I was not getting out of the car in that weather. Soon Jampot had clambered down the rocks and was out of sight. Perhaps when he reached the sea I would catch sight of him. He was up to his old tricks. However much I strained to look through the murky storm, there was no sign of him. The car rocked as the wind beat against it. The sea rose and fell, crashing in angry wild motions, pounding the rocks. Surely he could not survive swimming in these conditions. The water must be icy cold. What if he drowns or gets thrown against the rocks? What if he dies? I look down at the neat pile of clothes on his seat beside me. Is this the last I will see of him? It is laughable, but I'm not laughing, I'm terrified. I wouldn't know how to drive his sports car. I wouldn't know how to find my way home. My dyslexia is most evident when I am dealing with visual space. I never know where I am unless I have driven over the same route many times and my brain has understood the correlation between reality and the map in my head. I scour the sea, the horizon, the rocks and cliffs. No, nothing, only the storm which continues to batter everything I can see. How long should I wait before I go for help? We are parked off the road in a very isolated area. No one will find me here. I hate him for putting me through this fear again. I'm not sure where we are. Up north, yes, but where exactly? I try to open the car door. The wind pushes against it, howling at me. I haven't got the strength and give up. Part of the fear in me is released into anger and a desire to kill him.

Suddenly, without any warning, the car door is wrenched open. Jampot stands there grinning. His body is dripping wet and blue. Again, with dexterity unseemly of such a large man, he manages to get in the car and change into dry clothes, his damp body making it more of a struggle this time.

As we resume the drive home I am not in the mood for conversation. He soon picks up the grim vibes I emanate. His discomfort at the atmosphere I have produced is reflected in his driving. He pushes the car to go too fast, is reckless. My memories of our Spanish holiday return, haunting me as we hurtle through the countryside. Whatever made me think that I could deal with his erratic state of mind, his way of trying to control through fear? Every muscle in my body feels tight with tension. I do not think that relating this tale to mother will make her laugh, that is if I live long enough to tell her. Jampot is silent and his face has a fierceness that concerns me. Driving through the narrow country lanes at such speed makes my heart race. Now we are climbing a steep hill, at the crest we are going over 80 miles an hour. As we descend the other side it is like a downhill racetrack. Suddenly he throws the gear stick into neutral and we career down the slope. I can't look at the speedometer. I cling to the door. I'm petrified.

'This is it,' I swear to myself. 'I won't go on anymore with this lunatic. This really is the end.'

I am trying to calm myself down. I feel his driving go smoother as we try to have a kind of tentative conversation. Just when I thought we had passed the worst he has one more trick up his sleeve. We approach another steep hill. Jampot accelerates again and pops the car into neutral at the crest, only this time as we roar down the hill he lets go of the steering wheel with his hands and starts to steer with his knees. He unravels some dental floss, winding it around his fingers and starts to floss his teeth.

Sometimes you just have to pray.

It didn't end with a bang. Our relationship drifted on for a little while, breaking up more and more along the way. It was a disintegrating thing, stumbling uncomfortably to its end. When we reached it we both felt relieved to walk away.

*

"Is that Esther Fairfax?" the woman on the phone asked. "I'm putting on a course at Newbury College and we would like to invite you to take part."

I let her carry on, not knowing what this was about, not understanding.

"It's a Women in Management course."

Management? What do I know about management? It was a bewildering conversation. All I seemed to say was, 'Yes,' and 'Ummm.'

"Ros will be running it and we would love you to take one of the weeks and give us more understanding on how women can look after their health in their stressful lives."

I still wasn't sure exactly what was expected of me but I could feel an excited tingle running from my feet to my brain.

"Thank you, I would love to," I replied.

And so a new chapter in my life began.

I suggested to Ros that I attend the other classes on the course. Really, I badly needed to know what it was all about. I was going to be a tutor after all, whatever that meant. I had so much to learn.

I loved the classes and soon picked up what to do. After the six week course came to an end we had a party and a few of us have stuck together ever since. We meet regularly every month and have done for over 20 years. Ros was offered another course for the over-60s, this one on general life changes. She was too busy and asked me to take it. She also suggested that I take my City and Guilds 730 for the adult teaching certificate.

Apart from the six-week course I hadn't been to a class since I was 15 and I hated it then. Now I am over 50 and more excited than I could ever imagine. At first it isn't easy to understand what I am learning; it feels like a different language.

I feel like a real grown up in the real world and I love it. I'm writing essays, doing role-plays, being videoed. I feel stimulated and realise that I never have used my brain in this way before, not at school, not as a wife. I love it. I love it so much that I can't get enough of it. And so starts another career. I run regular courses at Newbury College and a subsidiary one in the next town, as well as evening classes and weekend workshops on assertiveness. This last one is, of course, a laugh. I am the least assertive person I know, but I know how to teach it.

With the extra money from teaching coming in and with a paying lodger I am racing towards paying off the mortgage. My exercise classes are doing well. Life feels full of meaning, of purpose. It is hard for me to believe that there was a time when I wanted to end it. It is even hard to believe that I had an eating problem. I am enjoying cooking good, healthy meals and inviting friends around. Even mother and I are doing okay. Of course she likes to have a dig at me here and there. Some of the assertiveness techniques I learned help a lot in how I handle her sharp tongue, even though I still find it quite difficult to be assertive with people in authority.

Jampot has at last given up on phoning me for a chat. I meet another man. Another romance is on the horizon. It does not last long this time though. I had done it again, falling for a controlling man, but this time I saw the signs and did not try to make it work. I join a dating agency. I think that this might help me get over my shyness and the hindrance to dating that comes from the fact that, due to the nature of my work, I live more in a woman's world. The dating agency experience causes great amusement to my lodger Rosemary and mother. My sons are less enthusiastic, more anxious. Where will this latest adventure take me? Most of the men I meet through the agency want to marry me. I hope that I let them down lightly. My confidence grows with all the compliments and flattery that my dates shower on me. Unfortunately I have to admit to myself that it is not really me they want. They need someone: anyone. I am not sure what any of them would have done if I had said yes to them. They did help me to see how good my own life is and show me that I do not need to be saved.

Yet love still found me. He was a friend at work, or so I thought. Slowly, with great gentleness, he slipped into my heart. I knew he was married and therefore kept my feelings to myself. I don't think I even mentioned them to Rosemary or mother. He was a secret that I was even trying to hide from myself. When you know something isn't possible it is easier not to admit it to yourself.

One day I was alone in the office, getting on with a mountain of photocopying. My mind was in a daydream as the machine went on laboriously sending out one copy after another. I became aware of someone standing behind me, very close behind me. I spun round and in the best romantic novel way found myself in his arms. He held me tight and we kissed. For the next couple of weeks we fought against our feelings, trying to deny they existed. He certainly didn't want to start an affair. He was a loyal and moral man. His principles were being tested. I had nothing to lose. I comforted myself, as I cried on the shoulders of friends. I was telling myself, and them, that I must hold back. This felt so unfair. He was such a lovely person. He had a heart of gold, was humorous and intelligent. He made me laugh and now all I do is cry. It seemed so unfair to meet a really special person and then have them remove themselves from your life. Oh yes, he'd told me about his sad and barren life with his desperate and needy wife who couldn't survive without him. Oddly enough, I was still so innocent I believed it all. Who knows, perhaps it was all true, or true enough for him to believe.

The agony of having to separate ourselves yet still work

together under the same roof got too much and we caved in one day. This began a most beautiful romance. I think that at last I might have broken my pattern of falling for controlling men. I did find that there are many delightful aspects of having a romance with a married man. For a start it felt a touch naughty, which added spice to our meetings. There was no chance of us committing to anything more than our love for each other. I enjoyed knowing that what we had was just in that moment. There were no ties, no duties, just a wonderful combination of lust and love. The poor man suffered a lot of guilt and conflict though. Happily, I didn't. Our relationship lasted many years. I suppose it was inevitable that it would destruct. His joy seemed always to be shadowed by his pain. I, on the other hand, grew bored. The very reasons for my delight in the early days became the reason for our relationship's decline. Knowing the relationship had nowhere to go was certainly attractive to me. Yet when it didn't go anywhere for so long, I grew bored. A relationship has to grow, to go through stages, and be able to develop. If this doesn't happen the relationship becomes one-dimensional and slowly dies. I finished it at this point.

Although I missed him dreadfully, I put all my energies into the work that was coming my way. I was learning all the advantages of living alone as well as how to accept the disadvantages. Once I got these straight my life moved on. There were moments of nostalgia, remembering afternoons spent in bed together with him and a bottle of wine, the thrill of anticipation before we would meet. I was grateful that I had so many memories to indulge in. These I could visit whenever I felt like, without ever growing bored, without anyone getting hurt.

Twenty

Mother in reflective mood.

I passed my City and Guilds certificate. It was the first thing I had passed in my life and I was so proud of myself. I was now qualified to teach adults. Wow. I got a real kick out of running the different classes: Personal Growth, Assertiveness and Life Skills. As I taught others I was learning so much.

Mother couldn't quite take it in that I was teaching subjects that had nothing to do with exercise but were about human interaction instead. I was still running the exercise classes as well. My newfound career was a part of my life that she wasn't able to identify with. Of course we both had so much in common otherwise. We could chat for ages about our studios; we both enjoyed talking work. We also had men and sex to talk about. The other parts of my life were as alien to mother as another planet. This wasn't harmful to our relationship. The areas we didn't connect in were in no way a threat to her competitive nature. All was smooth between us at this time though she still had her sharp tongue and put-downs. At least I had finally learnt to deal with these in such a way that it didn't turn into a drama and I felt less hurt by her, although I do not think that I felt hurt-free.

Since leaving John I am having more life changes than I expected to. I am delighted. I am enjoying every experience with such gusto for living. And now on the horizon appears my biggest life-change yet.

★

Mother is driving down tomorrow. She loves driving and visiting me. I always make sure I cook her favourite food and make enough for a doggie bag. She is very appreciative of all this. She knows what I cook will be easy to eat with her new teeth. Her teeth implants haven't been as successful as she had been led to believe they would be. Her body frequently tries to reject them and mother seems to live at the dentist. I get ready for her arrival. I have done all the shopping and most of the preparation. It is time to relax with a welcome cup of tea and settle down to read the local paper. I am thrilled to come across a photograph of my dear friend Sue, the Samaritan. I read on. She is being congratulated on becoming a director of the new Newbury branch of the Samaritans. The article mentions that the new branch is looking for recruits.

It has now been many years since Sue suggested to me that I would make a good Samaritan and to apply. The two years she recommended I wait in order to give my state of mind and emotions a chance to stabilise have lapsed. It had taken longer than I expected but now I feel ready. I was so excited as I dialled the number given in the paper. My hands were shaking.

"Hello, Samaritans, can I help you?"

All those years ago, that was the most comforting sentence to hear, now it was the most exciting. I explained that I wanted an interview in the hope that I might be recruited. Warm and friendly, the voice asked me for a few details. My interview was set up and directions were given. And that was that. When I told mother the next day she was unexpectedly nice about it. I was sure she would pooh-pooh it as she had done with my teaching at the college. But then, she had no idea what being a Samaritan would entail. Neither did I.

I was amazed and delighted to find that Sue was in charge of my interview. We had a great chat, partly I think, because she wanted to be sure that I wasn't still a needy mess. Being satisfied that I was okay, I went through a process called 'Selection'. After that I would eligible for the rigorous training. The selection day was held in Reading. Rosemary and I drove there together several times until I had learnt the way.

I had no idea what to expect. I arrived early and was so warmly welcomed by several Samaritans. I had the oddest feeling of having arrived home. I just knew deep down that this was where I belonged. I had arrived in the right place in the right time of my life. About 15 more recruits drifted in. We were offered coffee and biscuits and there was a slow and shy nodding in acknowledgement of each other. Bang on 10 o'clock we were pushed into a name game. This was followed by a trust game. And so the day passed, moving from one exercise to another, testing our awareness skills, our caring skills, our intuitiveness and our ability to listen. This was one of the most stimulating days of my life.

I drove home drained but bursting with feelings of excitement. I was told that a letter would follow in 10 days to let me know if I had passed. Rosemary and I had booked a holiday together in Corfu. The letter would undoubtedly arrive while we were away. Oh the pain, the agony of waiting drove me mad. I just had to be accepted. For the first time in my life I had found what I wanted to do, what I felt I was born to do. I must have driven Rosemary mad with my constant whine

of, 'I know I've been rejected, I know I'm not good enough.'
Poor Rosemary kept reassuring me that I would be fine but
nothing helped to calm me. The drive home from the airport
was silent. I rummaged through the mail the minute we got
back. There it was, an envelope with 'The Samaritans' written
on it. I shook as I opened it and promptly burst into tears as I
read the first sentence. Rosemary put her arms around me:

"Never mind, there'll be other things."

Sobbing, I said: "No, I've been accepted. Look, it says, we
are pleased to inform you ..." and I cried a bit more.

Rosemary hugged me.

The training was held in Reading. I learned telephone skills
I never knew I could, such as how to read someone's body
language over the phone. We can give and receive so much
information without even seeing each other, although there
is no substitute for having someone sitting opposite you so
you can absorb every expression, every almost-hidden movement and thought. Throughout the training I felt as if jump
leads had been attached to my brain. We went away on weekend workshops and I loved every second. Those sad and
withdrawn days of my school years were now truly made up
for. Learning was fun, fascinating, stimulating and incredibly
rewarding.

I was building lasting friendships and was enjoying a proper
social life. No longer having to worry about entertaining John
and his friends and drinking buddies, or any other man, was so
freeing. I was living my own life, one that I had carved out all
by myself. Soon I was climbing the Samaritan ladder. In the
Samaritans there are several groups of about eight or 10 people. The leader keeps an eye on the welfare of their designated
group as well as keeping ongoing training available. I became
leader of a group. Eventually I was asked to become a trainer

for new recruits. I was in my element. My teaching experience was now paying off in a way that I had not expected but was grateful for.

After a few years I realised that loving the work wasn't enough. More and more I found it frustrating that I was not allowed to do more than listen. I was not under any disillusionment about the importance of listening, especially after my own experience of needing the Samaritans' ear. I knew that listening was one of the greatest gifts you can give anyone. But still, I wanted more.

I had joined the Samaritans in 1986. Now, four years later, I decided that my next career move had to be to train as and become a counsellor. Which is exactly what I did. I loved the training but never felt comfortable writing the essays. I thoroughly enjoyed the hands-on work, the role-play, but putting what I was learning on paper was a struggle. It was hard for me to make what I wrote read like a sensible piece of knowledge expressed in a clever way. I came across as a dithering schoolgirl. I couldn't have been more surprised and delighted when I passed my assessment.

I continued running courses at the college and started private courses from my home as well as slowly building up a client base for my counselling practice. My mortgage was shrinking fast. After four enjoyable years, my lodger Rosemary left. She married and soon had twin sons. In the meantime I had some pleasant lodgers but there was one that stands out.

When he arrived I hardly heard his gentle knock at the door. He had rung the day before inquiring about my ad for a lodger.

"Please come in," I gestured, giving him my most welcoming smile whilst quickly summing him up.

He was tall, something over six foot, wearing a dark blue

business suit, white shirt and neat tie. His shoes gleam with years of polish. He carried a briefcase, indicating to me that he was a man of authority, someone well respected. I feel comfortable with him as we chat over a cup of tea and get the formal questions out of the way. We agree that he will move in the next week, on Monday. His soft voice and good manners reassure me that he is an honest Englishman.

It is my tradition to invite a new lodger to dinner on their first night as a relaxing way to break the ice and get to know each other. When I suggest this he immediately offers to bring the wine. I like this man already and look forward to him moving in.

It is a week later and I am just putting the rice on when I hear his gentle knock. Smart and smiling, he enters, offering me the wine he's brought.

"Dinner will be ready in 20 minutes," I announce.

"That sounds wonderful," he beams. "Would it be alright with you if I changed first?"

I nod, delighted with his good manners.

A few minutes later I have poured the wine when I hear his footsteps. I look up towards the open-plan stairs that lead straight from the kitchen to the upstairs landing. I am ready to offer him his glass as he descends. As his feet come into view I am quite surprised to see that a man of his height should be wearing high heels. I become more surprised as more of him is revealed. Above the high heels I see black tights then a very mini miniskirt, a white T-shirt and a brightly spotted scarf tied prettily around his neck. I can hardly conceal my surprise. He looks worried. His expression is anxious as he looks at me.

"Is this bad news for you? I can change if you like."

"Not at all." I am more amused now than shocked.

I can take this in my stride, mostly with thanks to my

mother who had two affairs with transvestites. She had given me detailed accounts of these relationships. Although this new lodger's dress was unexpected, it was not something I was unfamiliar with. My counselling work had also helped me to understand. We got on fine from that first evening and it wasn't long before this lodger became my lover. It was a short-lived and interesting experience, one which mother revelled in.

My next lodger was easily the most handsome and quite a bit younger than me. He was leaving his wife and wanted some space before moving in with the girlfriend he had started an affair with. It wasn't long before his desire for space and time turned into cuddles and good friendship with me. We would go to the pub together, stay up late talking, discussing, and cuddling some more. Which would it be for him? Would he go back to his wife who had started to feel jealous not only of the girlfriend but of me as well? Or would he move in with his girlfriend who had also started being jealous of me? I was highly amused as I was years older than this gorgeous lodger and had absolutely no designs on him apart from enjoying his kisses and cuddles. He enjoyed our relaxed flirtation. Eventually he came to the decision to move in with his girlfriend.

It is in part thanks to these lodgers that I was soon able to pay off my mortgage. They also provided so much rich life experience and good friendship.

I was now visiting my mother most weekends, bringing her prepared meals that would last at least part of the week. I also did a bit of shopping and cleaning for her. It was becoming obvious that she needed my help and was not coping very well with everything anymore. This was most apparent with her erratic driving. I didn't know how to approach her about it but it was getting more and more of a problem. Sometimes when driving down narrow streets with cars parked on both sides she would go at a snail's pace.

"You have to be so careful, you never know when a cat is sitting under a car and will suddenly run out in front of you," she explained.

The cars behind her would lose patience, honking their horns and getting out of their cars to shout abuse. Other times she would put her foot down at a red light and drive right through it. Sitting with her in the car terrified me. One weekend she wanted to come down and stay with me. I wasn't overly worried. The M4 stretches out with no cats around and no traffic lights to beat. Nevertheless, when mother arrived she was shaking and hot. I made her comfortable and gave her a weak cup of coffee just as she liked it, containing four spoonfuls of sugar. Mother admitted that this time, driving had scared her:

"Everyone drives far too fast; they are such a danger on the road. I had to drive on the hard shoulder all the way here to keep out of their way."

"That's it," I said. "Promise never to drive down to Hungerford again. From now on bring a friend who can drive you down and stay for the day."

Thankfully that is what she did from then on.

My next trip to London was with a friend. He was a gentle, kind, interesting man who was my first entirely platonic relationship with a person of the opposite sex. I was enjoying it. Mother wanted to meet him. She was finding it difficult to believe that any man and woman could have a wholly platonic relationship.

"It's just not normal," she repeated over and over again.

My friend was equally intrigued at the prospect of meeting

my mother. He wanted to meet this famous and charismatic woman that I still feared.

We had been to a matinee and had promised mother that on our way home we would pop in. After a few minutes with her I could see that my friend was being beguiled by mother's flirtations and outrageous questions. Mother was playing the coquette. After a while she offered us coffee. I followed her into the kitchen, offering to help. I noticed her body language was decidedly cool. Later that evening when I was back home mother rang.

"How could you treat me like that?"

My heart sank. How often have I had these phone calls, enduring the frosty low voice of her barely contained anger? Each time I received one of these phone calls from out of the blue I never knew what I had done wrong, what had triggered it. I had been under the impression that mother had rather enjoyed flirting with an attentive and intelligent man. I, foolishly, had believed that the visit had gone well.

"You humiliated me. You made me feel like a servant. A servant!" her voice rose. "A servant in my own home. How could you? I have never felt so humiliated. And by my own daughter! And you call yourself a counsellor. I dread to think what harm you do. You, who are supposed to have been trained to care, you couldn't care less for my feelings," she ran out of breath.

I was still none the wiser about what exactly I had done, although I was growing increasingly more curious. What could produce such a tirade? Eventually, when mother got her second wind and another wave of vitriolic words gushed out at me I started to make sense of it. It appeared that what caused all this was the fact that I had allowed her to make the coffee when really it was my place to do so. This was really too stupid for words. It didn't make sense. I was fed up of receiving phone calls from her, of allowing her to vent her venom on me.

I made a decision to no longer stay for a full weekend when I went to visit her, thinking it was better to keep these get-togethers short and sweet. I had had enough. My intention was to keep the visits full of laughter. She always liked me to clean her bath every time I came as it hurt her back to do so. I also would do a bit of shopping for her. I was only too glad to help with these little tasks to help make her life a little easier. These shorter visits worked well and we both were able to enjoy each other's company more. Mother certainly was behaving in a more loving way. Perhaps she was seeing the light: be nice to me and I'll be nice to you. She was less interested in taking her classes now, although she was always going to her studio. Her principal love affair now was with her beloved students. After class she would join a select few for a coffee. This became the highlight of her social life. Lois was the one who was keeping the studio running. More and more I could see that mother wanted to let go but couldn't bear to. Her studio was her baby. What could she do? Before long she made a huge decision and announced to one and all that she was retiring.

Nothing is ever cut and dried though, and mother's intention of retiring was mixed with confusion. For years and years she had proclaimed that she was a black and white person, that there were no greys in her life. Compromise was never an option, not with work, not with lovers, not with family. Black was her favourite colour. Her hair was always died jet black, she always drove a black car and even her eyes were black. I can't imagine the inner conflict and struggle she must have been going through in her attempt to retire. How could she let go of what had become so central to her life, her identity? Life was no longer black and white. Mother's emotions moved through anger, resentment and utter sadness. She couldn't bring herself to leave her studio alone, even after she had given it to Lois. Every morning she would go to one of the classes and pull one of her favourite students out and take her for a coffee. When she wasn't doing this, mother made Lois's life difficult by constantly going around the class and correcting the students or changing the exercises.

Mother started to phone me every day, sometimes twice a day:

"I feel so unwanted in my studio," she complained.

"But it's not your studio anymore," I would try to explain.

"What do you mean it is not my studio? Of course it is. How can you say that it's not mine, it's got a big sign outside saying, 'Lotte Berk Studio'. It's my life. Of course it's mine," her voice got louder and more agitated.

"No, mother. You sold it to Lois. Lois is being kind letting you come every day."

"Kind!" she shouted down the phone. "Kind? Have you gone mad? It is MY studio. Mine!"

I couldn't get through to her. I didn't know how to. What had she expected once she announced she was retiring and had sorted out a financial settlement with Lois? Thankfully, mother had changed her will back in my favour some while ago, apart from the studio, of course. I was glad. I could never have coped with running it, nor did I ever want to live in London again. But even more than that, Lois deserved the studio. She had worked for mother for years and given her heart and her soul to the studio and the students who all loved her so. She was brilliant at the exercises and had such a warm-hearted personality. I never did understand how Lois coped with mother's harsh tongue. Mother's black side never seemed to penetrate Lois's golden heart. Mother did love her and really appreciated her lovely personality.

I do not think that she ever really meant any harm to Lois, despite how much mother enjoyed hurting others. Every man who fell for mother was a worthwhile target. Hilde, mother's sister was a favourite as well. Lucky me, I used to think, I am the last in the firing line. But once father moved to Berlin and Hilde found love at last at the age of 69 and moved to Norfolk, I was moved to the front. Now that mother was almost 80 she didn't have any lovers to take the heat either. That left me. By now I was learning to handle her knife throwing sessions, deftly side stepping the bigger attacks.

For her 80th birthday her students arranged a big party. She rang, dying to tell me all about it, delighted with the fuss that was being made over her.

"I want to wear something that gives me dignity and style. I don't know what to do. Should I buy a new outfit or wear one of my handmade suits?" her voice had an excitement that had been lacking lately.

She rattled on, thrilled that at last something was happening in her life, which had recently been so dull for her. I fear she was also suffering from loneliness, even though she refused to admit it. She needed to feel adored, respected, admired for herself, but, oddly enough, not for her exercises. As our conversation neared an end she said:

"I am sorry darling but you are not invited."

I thought that this was odd as I have always got on well with her students whenever I saw them.

"Of course." she continued. "If it was up to me I'd ask you, but it is not in my hands. They don't want you to be part of my celebration."

I wasn't in the least upset as I didn't actually believe her. Of course, it may well have been the truth, but we'll never know.

On reflection I question the possibility that this was one of the early signs of dementia. No one else seemed to notice. Mother was known for being unpredictable and frequently eccentric. As for me I couldn't quite understand her exaggerated behaviour and way of playing with the truth. I just put it down to her getting older. The brain damage that was darkly moving in and taking over wasn't yet obvious enough to recognize so nothing was said or done. The only area where I tried to put my foot down was her driving. When I suggested to her that she was becoming a dangerous driver and that the time had come to give up she flew into a rage.

"You want me to give up my last pleasure in life. You expect me to use public transport? Are you mad? I suppose you think I am so rich that I can afford to go everywhere by taxi?"

I never dared mention it again. Mother continued to drive around London, most likely with chaos in her wake. I did, however, make it quite clear that when I visited her I would not let her drive me anywhere. On my visits we were restricted to finding local cafes and restaurants in Shepherd's Bush. There were plenty of really nice places to choose from. Luckily her favourite Indian restaurant was opposite her home at The Grampians.

For two years Lois put up with Lotte's increasingly difficult and disruptive behaviour in the studio. Eventually the time came when Lois was almost at breaking point and she decided to sell the studio on to a French student who excelled in the exercises and was longing to get her hands on it. This new owner began by also being kind to mother whenever she appeared. Mother was becoming a raging inferno of feelings and she made even more trouble than previously in the classes.

"The teaching here is awful. Don't come here again," she would exclaim to the students.

She would also snatch the phone whenever it rang and

whether it was a student wanting to book, or an inquiry for classes, mother would rant down the phone.

"Don't come here, this is a dreadful place!"

It wasn't long before the French girl couldn't take any more. She asked mother not to come to the studio. Mother wouldn't listen and continued on her vendetta. Eventually a lock was put on the door, which needed a combination to open. In her frustration and anger mother removed the 'Lotte Berk Studio' sign from the front of the building and never went back there again. It really was the end, even though mother was swearing that it was her studio still. Of course it was, really. She had made it, built it up, loved it. It would always be hers.

Twenty-one

Mother in care home, 2000.

I visited mother every weekend. However much she denied it, I felt her loneliness. Without her studio, her routine, and her daily laugh with the girls, her life was empty. She phoned me every night. We would watch the same TV programme while we chatted, occasionally commenting on what we were watching. It made evenings less lonely for her. Every Sunday father would phone her from Berlin. These calls meant so much to her; they made her feel that there was still a man in her life. He had always loved her and told her so. She needed to hear that now more than ever. She also needed my love and needed me to express it constantly. A few years ago I would have balked at this. At last I was growing up and, thanks to my work in counselling, had a far greater understanding of the human condition. Because of this I was able to open my heart to her genuinely.

My father always tried to visit me once a year, when he visited his ex-wife and son. He would make the journey from Germany to England on his beloved motorbike. Sometimes I would go to London and spend the day with mother and father together. We would go out as a threesome. I couldn't help but smile to myself. We must have looked a lovely, loving family as we sat together in the Conditori in Queen's Way, stuffing German sausages (father, a vegetarian, had potato salad) and cake into our laughing faces. We reminisced about the ghost rides of our lives, happy to have survived them and to still be smiling.

My father's last visit to see me on his motorbike was over a Christmas holiday. He was 81. The weather had been icy and Europe was frozen. Father loved the heat and needed to feel warmth. This must have been a tough journey for him as his old bones rattled through Germany and all of France until he reached the channel ferry. He never liked to stop off if he could avoid it. His arrival in England was foggy and ice bound, it had been a hard winter. By the time he got to my house it was dark. I heard the throb of his motorbike as he gave the throttle a last blast and killed the engine. I ran out to greet him, amazed and proud of his achievement. He swung his legs off the bike. They stayed in a wide arc as if he was straddling an imaginary motorbike. His arms were similarly stuck in a semi circle as if he was holding the handlebars. As he walked towards me swinging himself in an almost John Wayne-like swagger, an exaggerated Michelin man, he said:

"Sorry, Liebschen, I can't hug you yet, I'm frozen stiff in this position."

A year after this visit he had his first stroke. After this, even he had to admit that it was time to give up his beloved motorbike. He replaced it with an old, rattling, rusty Renault 5. He never liked or respected cars.

Father was always excellent at making friends. Now that he had settled in Berlin, he had a good support network so I did not need to worry so much about him. A year after his first stroke he had another. The next year, 1996, three weeks before his 84th birthday, he died. Since then his life and work has been well documented in Germany, especially his modern dancing, mime, and interpretations of poetry, as well as his electronic compositions. He was always well ahead of his time. Although I feel emotionally distant from him I am also exceedingly proud of him. I hold a fondness for him, despite it all.

His death left another empty space in mother's life. Now there was no man, no studio. Even her sister had died, the year before my father. I was now her everything. I was the only one left who knew her through and through, knew her history, her dramas. It wasn't that she didn't have any friends. She certainly did have friends, friends who loved her. But when it came down to it, I was it, the bottom line, just as my sons are for me. No one knows me better.

Meanwhile, in my own life, my neighbours were stressing me more and more. On one side a family with countless children ranging from teenagers to a baby moved in. It was a cold winter and they had not had a chance to sort out their heating. I offered them an old electric heater to help them through. Thank goodness I had. Unbeknownst to me this had been an extremely good move as during their time in our neighbourhood many of the cars were spray painted with graffiti. I couldn't understand why mine had been conspicuously left alone when everyone else's had been vandalised. Weeks later the penny dropped. Apart from this, to say that their language was colourful would be an under-statement. Thanks to my Samaritan training I had heard every obscenity possible and so was not too shocked. I would look out of my back bedroom window each day in amazement as more and more garden furniture and children's playground equipment piled up in their garden leaving no space to even use it. So why was it there? I soon found out. An unmarked police car had them under surveillance. It wasn't long before the man of the house was arrested.

My neighbours on the other side had their own way of being vandals. The loud noise that throbbed from their house was invasive to me. They also left their animals locked up for days when they went away. Hearing their dog's howling whine broke my heart. Sadly I didn't get any help from the RSPCA who, when they came out to investigate, said that it was not cruelty but neglect and walked away. I'm still trying to understand where the line is between those two.

One day I smelt burning and ran to look out my back bedroom window and saw plumes of black smoke snaking across my garden. The boy next door had collected some of the furniture from inside his house and placed it into a big hole that he had dug in the garden. He then set the pile alight. Fire, it seemed, was a big attraction for the boy. Previously he had tried his hand at making homemade bombs using milk bottles. For me this was the last straw. The time had come for me to move.

I find that there is something delightful and heart-warming about discussing my thoughts and making decisions with a good friend over a bottle of wine.

"My neighbours are driving me mad," I confided in one such good friend as I poured our second glass of wine. "What do you think? Should I move? I had thought that I would try to hang on for another four years or so before I moved but the neighbour on one side has been stealing faster than a thieving magpie and the ones on the other side are breeding a pyromaniac. Perhaps I should consider moving sooner, maybe in two years instead."

"Why wait?" came the sensible reply.

"I thought I could be saving up for a bigger mortgage."

"That's crazy," my dear friend exclaimed. She leant forward and with a wagging finger:

"Go to the estate agent's tomorrow; don't waste time. I'll give you the name of an excellent and honest agent. I want to hear from you that you have done as I have told you."

She was always a bit like that, but she was right. The next morning I went to see the recommended estate agent and before I could say, 'I'm in no hurry,' my house was put on the market. I felt frighteningly insecure. In my mind, I should have found a house first and then put mine up for sale. I was assured that the best way was for me to start looking now.

On my next visit to London mother and I started off with coffee at Cafe Rouge, where I told her about my plans. We always went to the loo together and I noticed, not for the first time, that she no longer washed her hands but instead sprayed them with perfume, rubbing them together as if with soap. I put it down to her becoming more eccentric now that she was in her eighties and that it was only to be expected. We walked up to the Indian restaurant for lunch. I was sticking to my resolve to not let mother drive me around London. Sometimes she grumbled at me for my stubbornness.

"I just don't understand why you won't come in the car with me. I am such a safe driver, not fast like you."

I ignored these grumbles and continued to talk about my decision to move. She liked to be involved in my thoughts and plans. She asked me questions about my ability to take such a big step and the wisdom of such upheaval. She really had been listening. During the week that followed she seemed to have done some serious thinking because the next weekend as we sat once again over coffee at Cafe Rouge she announced that she would like to move to Hungerford. I was aghast. Mother had always made it clear how she hated the countryside and thought anyone who lived there didn't have a brain, unless of course they also had a place in London as well. She had always sworn that she would never leave London.

Part of me was quite excited at the thought of mother living nearby. Part of me thought that nothing could be worse. The voice of that psychiatrist came back to me once again, 'Never live close to your mother.'

But surely now I could manage any difficulties I would have with her. Surely by now I had grown up more and mother had mellowed. I put all these thoughts out of my head and concentrated on the fact that this was just what she needed and that it could be nice for me, too, as long as we put down a few ground rules.

Mother was so thrilled and excited that she agreed to all of the ground rules I proposed. The first of these was that she had to agree to give up driving. She really didn't know her way around our country lanes and would have found it all too confusing. She agreed with no hesitation. This was all going very well.

A couple of days later mother phoned me in the afternoon. This was quite unusual as she liked to save our chats for the evening. She sounded agitated.

"Someone's been in my flat," she sounded half frightened, half angry.

"How did they do that? You have so many locks on your door; it would have been difficult for them to break in."

"No, no, they must have had a key. The door is fine."

"What's missing?" I asked.

"It's very odd. My Whistles suit is missing and the thieves exchanged it for a Marks and Spencer suit. It is hanging up in exactly the same place as my Whistles one. Who would do such a thing?"

That's more than a bit odd, I thought. Heavens, she's becoming more and more eccentric. And still I did not sense that it was anything more than that. The following weekend when I went up to visit she was full of her plans to move and very happy, excited that something was happening in her life.

"I'm going to leave it up to you to find me a place. I know that whatever you think is nice I will love."

So it was left up to me to find her new abode as well as finding my own.

I am a great telly addict and love watching shows on how to do up your house or what best tactic to use to give your home sale appeal. One particular programme had ideas that seemed to make sense to me. I was already a bit of a minimalist so I didn't need to unclutter my house like they suggested, and it is always clean and tidy thanks to my cleaner Beanie who kept it looking perfect. Music would help to bring a sense of peace and tranquillity as well; I would just have to hope that the neighbours were out. The programmes also suggested putting a pot of coffee on so that the smell could waft through the house as most people respond to it.

Now I was set for my first viewing. I waited, nervously pacing up and down. There was a stillness in the air, a silence seldom heard with neighbours like mine. My prayers had been answered; they must have been out destroying the world elsewhere that day. I placed a cassette in the player and soon the gentle sound of Handel gave the house an even more hushed air. The coffee was on and smelled tempting.

This was my first experience of showing someone around my house. Myself, I get very put off when a salesperson tries to convince me of the excellence of an object, when they point out the obvious and don't give me credit for my own intelligence. Car salesmen are at the top of my hate-list for this. As I wait for the first viewing, my own sales plan is all in place:

no pushy pitch, let them ask questions, give them lots of space as they wander around.

It all went more easily than I ever expected and the next day they put in an offer for the asking price. One down now, only two more to go. I had to get out and find a house for me, and a flat for mother.

I don't like stress and I don't know how to deal with it. I had been on a stress management course before but it didn't seem to include what I was experiencing. I was not prepared for the stress of buying two homes at once, dealing with other people's chains as well as coping with mother.

I visited every estate agent in Hungerford searching for a four bedroom house.

"No, we've nothing like that, the market isn't moving much."

But I needed to move, and much sooner than expected. It so often happens that the last place you look, you find your dream. Not that I knew that it was my dream. I had just about given up when I walked into the last estate agent's office. The estate agent was out and his overworked secretary was glued to her computer. I told her what I wanted.

"No, nothing like that on the books at the moment. The market is quite dead. Although, having said that, we do have this delightful three bedroom house with the most amazing views."

She pulled the information about it from the file of hundreds of houses that were stranded in some no-mans-land of unsalable properties.

"I really am looking for four bedrooms ... ' I start to say but just as she slides the details back into their folder I catch a glimpse of a photograph of the house. "I suppose it wouldn't hurt to look at it."

She locked the office and I followed her up the street to the house. The biggest task when viewing houses is learning how to look beyond the current resident's taste. I strained to see beyond the thick nylon carpets, the thick curtains that were half drawn and then tied back. Every surface, even the landing windowsill, was adorned with knick-knacks. The first thing that I was pleased to see was the cat flap, which would please my cat as well. And the bathroom had a bidet. I always said that my next house would have a bidet, half-joking. The house was quite unprepossessing. It was built in the mid-1970s and you could hardly call it your castle. But something hit me about it. Was it instinct? I don't know, but it felt so right that I could feel a buzz of electricity run through my veins. My heart beat faster and the feeling of those first stages of falling in love embraced me.

Of course it was much more than I could afford. I put in a ridiculous offer of £10,000 less than the asking price. I was, quite naturally, turned down but then told that they would accept £5,000 less than the asking price. Once again, raising a bigger mortgage at my age was not going to be easy. Luckily the angels were smiling on me. One of my clients worked in the mortgage business and got me a fantastic deal. I was now the proud owner of a 25 year mortgage at the grand age of 63. I would be 88 when I paid it off. What utter madness. I'm not even sure I'm going to live that long. Yes, I got a lodger. I was determined to be free of the mortgage as soon as possible.

Now I needed to find a home for mother and her cat. I had noticed over the past few months that her flat had started to smell badly and it was getting worse. I couldn't work out where it was coming from. Was it that she didn't clean out the cat litter frequently enough? It was an odd smell, quite distinctive. It was being partly masked by mother's new ritual of squirting and even pouring perfume over herself and most other places as well.

"What is that dreadful smell?" I asked her one weekend.

"What smell?" she replied.

"Oh come on, mother, don't tell me you can't smell this disgusting smell."

"I can't smell anything. I just think you want to be horrid to me."

"Mother, I can hardly breathe in here it is so awful."

"Well, if it is so awful don't stay here."

I realised we were getting nowhere.

I moved into my new house in May, 1998, after having found the ideal place for mother in April. She would be living in a perfect ground floor flat in a sheltered home just off the High Street. It would be easy for her to pop into the hotel across the road for the coffee and Danish as she always had done in London. It would be good for her to enjoy the same routine here in Hungerford.

Mother moved into her new flat in June along with her cat, which she wasn't actually permitted to have. Luckily the warden felt honoured to have the famous Lotte Berk living under her roof and I think she would have allowed mother anything she wanted. Mother had one friend already then, so things were getting off to a good start.

For the first week of mother's life in Hungerford I went to see her every day. I showed her the shops and we would go out for lunch. That was part of the rules we had agreed, that I would visit frequently while mother settled in and then I would tail off the visits, bringing her back to my house occasionally to cook her favourite meals for her. I also found her a cleaner.

Mother must have felt at home. She started to be critical

about everything. The first cleaner that I found had too much grey hair. The second's bottom was too large. The third talked too much. I gave up. I found myself starting to become more and more frustrated and irritated. There was no pleasing her. One day she was being particularly scratchy and difficult.

"I don't want to live in the country anymore. I have decided to move back to my flat in the Grampians."

"Mother, I hardly think that is possible," I pointed out.

"Of course it is possible, it is my flat!"

"Not anymore, you gave it up," I tried to explain.

"Well, I can get it back!" she snarled at me.

I hadn't expected this and was stuck for an answer that she would understand. Meanwhile, her lovely little Hungerford flat had started to smell as bad as the one in London. There was no convincing her that it did, though, and even the cleaners were unable to get rid of the smell. Sometimes it felt like this repulsive odour was stuck in my nose and seemed to be everywhere.

*

I could smell mother so strongly as I walked into Boots. Her perfume lingered in my nostrils, a mix of unwashed body with a hint of urine. I looked up and down the aisle. Surely she must be here. Yet there was no sign of her. I did my shopping and went to pay.

"Oh, you've just missed your mother," the assistant said.

Click, click, click. I could hear the sound of her walking stick before I could see her. It wasn't really a walking stick; it was one of those sticks with a metal end that you can manoeuvre to pick things up off the floor. Mother preferred this to a conventional walking stick. Even to this day whenever I hear a metal tipped walking stick click against the pavement I am left with a sinking feeling of dread. It is amazing how noises and smells can bring back memories. Like lightning I can be transported to where I do not want to go, back to the well trodden path of sadness as I watched mother's decline into dementia.

I didn't really see it happening at first, it was all so gradual and punctuated with such perfect lucidity. She was naturally eccentric which meant she got away with odd behaviour for a long time before anyone realised anything was wrong. It was her phone calls that made me start to feel more and more concerned. She began ringing frequently and often in the middle of the night.

"Is it time for me to go to the hairdresser?" mother asked.

"No, it is two a.m., it is night-time. Look out the window and you will see that it is dark outside."

Another time she rang:

"Are you coming to join me for coffee and a Danish at the hotel, darling?"

Again I had to explain that it was the middle of the night.

If that wasn't stressful enough for me, I decided to build an extension to my house. I had been running my classes in my sitting room, pushing the little furniture that I had to one end. Now I was going to make the room larger and lighter. A one-man-band builder had been recommended to me. He did a grand job and I never had to close a class. He managed to build the extension around us, to the great amusement of the class and to his great pleasure.

Although this builder was good, no one has been as good to me as Ron, my handyman extraordinaire. He made my home the dream I visualized it could be. Every woman needs a Ron in their lives. I certainly could not have done without him. I first met him when he joined one of my assertiveness classes at the college. Whatever occurred during that course, it worked for Ron. His progress was so staggering that I put him up for student of the year. I became friends with him and his wife. Before long, Ron, who was working as a caretaker at an old person's home, started doing odd jobs around my house. He helped me move into this house, decorating it and installing ballet barres around the sitting room for my classes. He knocked down a wall in my bedroom, making it into the beautiful big room that I now so enjoy. Eventually I encouraged him to start up his own business doing all those jobs that husbands try to get out of. This has been a huge success for him.

Meanwhile my nice young Scottish lodger left me to move to London. My next lodger was a terrific girl. Even though I was 18 years older than her, we were like twins at heart. She became my best lodger ever. The light relief that she brought into my life was exactly what I needed after all of the upheaval and change. We went on shopping sprees, drinking sprees. I lost my fear of alcohol. For so long I had been so terrified that I would become an alcoholic if I had more than two drinks. Not anymore. We giggled our way through bottles of wine.

Mother impressed me with how well she was settling into her new life. She built a familiar routine for herself. Every morning she would take a gentle stroll to the hotel opposite her home. There, she would always get a warm welcome. The staff delighted in her eccentric conversation and always made her feel special by bringing her favourite cappuccino and Danish without her having to order it. I would frequently meet her there in an attempt to avoid having to go into her smelly flat. It was good to see how much attention she was getting from the waitresses. Yet it was still depressing to see how rapid she was in decline. Despite the apparent order of her days, I had to face facts. There was no doubt that mother was becoming more confused. I decided that a visit from the doctor would help to clarify the situation for me and help me find out how best to take the next steps.

The doctor dealt with mother gently and with the patience and understanding that I felt I lacked. I hated myself for this. It was all so hard. The doctor referred mother to a psychiatrist who tested her memory. This was followed later by a brain scan.

"I can tell you now, Mrs. Fairfax," the psychiatrist said with that I-know-what-I'm-talking-about-voice. "Your mother will have to go into a nursing home. Perhaps she will manage another six months as long as carers are in daily. She has had many mini strokes. The scan showed up some areas of her brain which have died."

The next six months became darker by the day. I found my-self almost lost in her confusion. I didn't understand the disease that was taking my mother from me. What exactly did dementia mean? How could I help her? My friends and my sons were loving and supportive but that still didn't help me understand what was happening to mother. The doctor advised me to apply for power of attorney and to talk to mother's bank manager. I didn't understand what this was all about but did as I was told.

The bank manager came to see mother in her smelly flat. I was so embarrassed but he took it in his stride. Mother adored him and they had built up a good relationship. Now he was trying to explain that signing the papers to hand her finances over to me was for her benefit. I could see that it made sense but I wasn't surprised when her eyes turned black and she burst out:

"Never, never will I let Esther get her hands on my money."

So, she had understood the gist of the conversation, a very lucid moment for her, indeed. Sadly she didn't see the good sense in allowing me to take charge of her affairs. The bank manager had been noticing that she had been taking out £400 a day from her account. We had no idea what she did with that money. Sensibly he proposed that a £50 limit on her daily withdrawals would be a good idea. Mother continued her rant:

"Esther would steal every penny from me. I would end up on the streets."

"Oh, I don't think so," the bank manager gently tried to talk sense to her.

"You don't know her, she wants my money."

I sat, horrified at her accusations and hoping that the bank manager would see through the nonsense that she was gushing out.

We gave up for the time being and he and I walked over to the bank to arrange the £50 limit. He assured me that he didn't think that I wanted to steal mother's money and suggested that I just left it to him to talk her around. He did have a point. The fact that he was a man was halfway to success already. I agreed. Before I knew it, like a gentle flowing river he had calmed her down and soon she was eating out of his hand. She signed the papers.

Twenty-two

Mother & me sharing a loving moment in the care home, 2002.

It was a quiet Sunday afternoon when the phone rang.

"I am calling to inquire about a woman, her name is Esther Fairfax."

The man had a deep voice with a hint of a Berkshire accent. I felt a chill creep over me. It was a strange way to start a conversation.

"Yes, that's me."

"You are Esther Fairfax?"

"Most definitely."

"Have you been hurt? Are you alright?"

"I'm fine. I haven't been hurt."

"You haven't been raped?"

"No, I certainly have not been raped."

This was a most surreal conversation.

"You haven't been mugged?"

"No. Please tell me what this is all about."

"I'm sorry if I've distressed you but we had to check this out, we follow up all emergency calls."

"Who are you? Are you the police?"

"No, Mrs. Fairfax, we are the backup emergency call centre

285

for the sheltered home that your mother is in. When the warden has a weekend off we're on call. We had a call from your mother a few minutes ago. She had pulled the emergency cord, which comes through to us so we can speak to her directly. I'm afraid she was quite hysterical and utterly convincing. She told us that you were lying on her bed in a pool of blood and that you had been mugged and raped. We were about to call the police but thought we'd check first. I'm glad we did and I'm glad you're okay."

"Thank you. I'll visit her straight away."

This was the first of a series of hallucinations.

I called the social services who spoke kindly to me as I sobbed down the phone:

"I can't cope anymore. I need help," I said.

I hated having to admit it but it was true.

The carers had a tough job with my mother. Sometimes she refused to let them in and instead would shout abuse at them through her letterbox. They would phone me with their complaints.

"It's not our job to clean the place. It's filthy and it smells."

"I know that it's filthy, that's why she needs help. She can't look after herself very well. Please help her. She needs care."

It was a situation that was spiralling out of control. Her hallucinations increased. She would frequently cry about the dead children that she could see bleeding as they hung from the doors. She told me of a close friend who was sleeping in her airing cupboard.

"Come, see," she would say, opening the cupboard door and gesturing in.

I was falling apart. One particular morning I was inconsolable. Sue begged me to call Marijke who was one of my most sensible and down to earth friends. I did. Marijke came round at once and marched me straight to the doctor's. My GP wasn't on duty so we met with the stand-in GP. Marijke explained the situation while I sat helpless with tears still streaming down my face.

"I could put her on a couple of pills," he suggested, nodding towards me.

If only I could have filmed the next few minutes. Marijke's voice, like cold steel, cut through the room:

"No, not Esther. Do something about her mother. Whose responsibility is this? It's yours, you have to do something about it today."

And he did.

He sent for an ambulance and arranged for mother to be taken to the nearest psychiatric hospital. My guilt as I watched her being put into the ambulance and driven away was the most painful I have ever felt. I had sent her to hell. I knew what hell that was because it was the very hospital where I had spent a year doing voluntary work as an occupational therapist. And now I had condemned my own mother to that fate. I was her jailor. I hated myself.

Despite this, I had a week of relative peace in which I patched myself up and got onto social services. I explained the situation and how mother was no longer able to stay in her sheltered flat as she had become disruptive to the other residents. She had been known to stand naked by her window, showing her body to everyone passing by. Social Services organised a most desirable nursing home for mother. It was only a five-minute drive from my house, as well. I do not know how they managed to fix it all so quickly; I had heard that they had a long waiting list. While last minute arrangements were made, mother was returned to her flat. This gave me a bit of time to figure out how I would convince her that she had to move. There was no way she was going to understand that she had no choice in the matter.

While sipping a cup of tea in bed, I had an idea. A hotel, of course, was the answer. Mother loved them. On our last trip abroad, to Cologne, a few years earlier, we had stayed in the Dom Hotel, opposite the Cathedral. Hitler was rumoured to have stayed there. It was an old fashioned place, and very stuffy, that cost the earth to stay in. I couldn't quite understand why she wanted us to stay there, until I experienced the outstanding service. Every thought was catered for before it was even voiced. This kind of pampering and attention had done wonders for mother. Now it struck me that the only way to sell the move to mother was to say that she would be going to a hotel. I couldn't see any other way of moving her.

I arranged with Ron for a few of her bits and pieces to be moved into her new room to give her a sense of familiarity. Lois came down from London on the day of mother's move. It would help to have a reassuring and friendly face to keep mother calm. As we drove into the grounds and parked the car mother took one look at the building and declared firmly in her deep voice, 'How working-class.' Well, it wasn't the Dom or the Churchill. It had that look of an institution that had tried to look more homely but had failed. My heart sank. Was this going to be the first sign of trouble from mother? 'Please don't be difficult,' I whispered under my breath.

It was about midday and we had been invited to stay with mother for lunch to help her settle in. As we walked towards the dining room a tall, straight-backed woman went in front of us. She had a frizzy mass of grey hair. Mother nudged me with her elbow and in a stage whisper said:

"Look, there's Beethoven!"

Well, what could be better than to be living under the same

288

roof as one of her favourite composers? Lunch was a reconstituted slab of meat, origins unknown, and lumpy mashed potatoes with dark gravy. We ate at a table with two other residents. As I sat there, barely able to eat the meal before me, I was appalled at the fate I'd consigned my mother to. When it was time to leave, she clung to me as I walked to the entrance.

"Don't leave me here, please, don't. Don't," she pleaded, with her fingers gripping my arm, holding me so tightly that I was unable to move. I tried explaining that I would be back tomorrow.

"No, no, you don't have to go. They have rooms and they don't charge. Please don't go."

Her pleas were breaking my heart. A helper came by and understood the situation at once. In a soft gentle voice she coaxed my mother to let go and then led her away down the corridor.

For the next year, after every visit mother tried to stop me leaving. We would go through the same performance: her clinging onto me, making it impossible to leave, her voice, begging me to stay. Only when a helper came to my rescue could I get out, but even then I could hear her shouting after me, 'Esther, Esther,' as she was led down the corridor. I had not expected to feel such pain on every visit. It soon became my habit to stop at my local supermarket on my way home. Not to shop. I would sit in the car park and cry my heart out. This stopover gave me time to return to my own world, to watch people doing normal things and to get a grip on myself before returning to my quiet home.

It was easier visiting mother when I had a friend with me. She seemed to enjoy it more, too. When my friends, Sue or Angela, and I went together we would take mother out to the local pub. Mother would be on orange juice and we would be on wine and a good laugh would be had by all. Mother's wicked remarks, made quite openly and not too quietly, gave us much to giggle about.

"Look," mother would remark. "That woman's bottom is fat like a pig's." She pointed at the poor woman, "I've got a face like that in my knickers."

That would be when we knew it was time to leave, before she became even ruder or before we were thrown out.

The best time of all was when Michael, Jo and I would visit her together. Even though mother did not seem to understand our hi-jinks she joined in our uncontrollable laughter as we pranced and mimed. At some level we were connecting with her and she was able to join in the fun. Still, she wasn't all there. One time she was convinced that Jo was her father, another time that he was Ernest. But after those jolly visits with the boys I never felt the usual sadness in my heart. We had seen that mother was still able to enjoy herself.

There was one visit I made with Jo, which he won't let me forget about. When we arrived the care home's lounge was full to bursting. Because it was a weekend there were more visitors than usual. The only place we could find to sit was on a sofa in the corridor. By this time mother was using a proper walking stick. As we sat happily chatting, mother was sneakily sticking her walking stick out whenever someone came past us. As they tripped and then recovered themselves they would look round to see what had caused them to stumble. Mother would look at them with a most concerned expression and say with her thick accent:

"Oh, I'm so sorry."

Then there would be smiles all around and they continued on their way. Mother would repeat this performance with the next passer-by. She would become convulsed with giggles and Jo and I were making efforts to swallow the laughter that was trying to escape our bodies. We'd look at each other with that knowing look. She might have lost a few marbles but certainly not her mischievous sense of humour.

But dementia doesn't stand still. It creeps ever forward. There is no getting better. Bit by bit it was eating mother's brain, robbing her month by month of her experiences, her wisdom, and her life's memories. She could still use words but no longer seemed to understand what was being said. She no longer clung to me when I went to leave. She no longer knew who I was.

"You know," she said to me as we walked arm in arm around the communal garden. "I have a daughter just like you."

I swallowed the lump in my throat that threatened to bring tears. I hugged her, hoping she could feel my love.

Another year went by, and another. Now she couldn't use language at all. Her only words are, 'aha, aha, aha.' Over and over again, all day long.

"Oh shut up," another resident shouts at her.

Anger bubbles up inside me. 'Don't shout at my mother like that.' I want to say, but don't. All the designer clothes that she brought with her have been ruined by the nursing home's laundry. Everything has to be boiled. Mother is now doubly incontinent, like many of the residents here. It was difficult to see mother wearing an acrylic cardigan, a dirndl skirt and fluffy pink slippers, her silk blouses boiled to oblivion, her Yves Saint-Laurent trousers and suits now shrunk and shredded in the wash. Now mother wears dead peoples' clothes. Another year and she will join them.

I feel it will be a blessed release for us both. For nearly five years she has been living like this: alive but not as someone I really knew. That charismatic, vibrant, intelligent, humorous woman was somehow left in London, the city she loved, when she moved to Hungerford. I had been given five years of borrowed time to help me come to terms with our conflicts of love and rejection. I could see that despite the pain it was a treasured gift.

As the end drew nearer mother slipped into a coma. I sat by her bedside, hardly able to recognize her yellow, shrunken body, her mouth stuck open like Munch's scream. If only I had the strength I could have put a pillow over her face to end her suffering. But that was completely impossible, even though I knew that that would have been what she wanted. Did I not love her enough to do it? Or, maybe after all, I loved her too much.

Mother died on the 4th of November, 2003. She is at peace now. So am I. Mother would have enjoyed her send off. The words I read at her funeral would have delighted her, they were George Constanza's Words of Wisdom from the American sit-com *Seinfeld*:

Life As It Should Be

'The most unfair thing about life is the way it ends. I mean, life is tough. It takes up a lot of your time. What do you get at the end of it? A death. What's that, a bonus? I think the life cycle is all backwards. You should die first. Get that out of the way. Then you go to live in an old age home. You get kicked out for being too healthy, go collect your pension, then, when you start to work, you get a gold watch on your first day. You work 40 years until you're young enough to enjoy your retirement. You drink alcohol, you party, you get ready for High School, you become a kid, you play, you have no responsibilities, you become a little baby, you go back, you spend your last nine months floating with luxuries like central heating, spa, room service on tap, then you finish off as an orgasm! Amen.'

The crematorium rocked with laughter and applause.

Twenty-three

Me enjoying a laugh in our garden.

I lie in wait, and I wait, and wait, and wait. No tears come. Not the first week. Not the first month. They will not come. Like snowflakes softly falling on skin, my emotions have such softness, such lightness as they are slowly released from the twisted bond they shared with mother. She is gone and with her all my stress, my anxiety, my worry and fear. Slowly I move on, hardly trusting how lovely life is feeling. It is almost as if I am waiting for my inner glow to be stamped on. But it is not. Instead it grows and grows in its brightness.

Every visit from Jo and Michael brings a fountain of compliments, 'Mother, you look so young, so beautiful.' They continue such compliments over the phone, in letters. I curl up inside with embarrassment, twist with discomfort, and burst with delight. They are seeing how I feel and I love it. If someone asked me what happiness is I could only answer with how I feel now. Every morning I wake up happy. Every night I go to bed happy. I have lost the fear that a shadow is creeping up on me. Possibly love has a big influence on this happiness I feel. I love my house. It is everything that I want it to be and in it I am as comfortable as someone in a most beloved pair of old slippers. I love my work, teaching mother's exercises, which brings laughter into my life each day. I love my friends, and so I should – I chose them. Most of all, I love my boys and feel their love.

I have the freedom to choose what I want from life and now, after so many years of struggle, I have my independence. I am not answerable to anyone else. Surely this feels better than any drug. I love being old. I love being single. I no longer live for others, either pleasing them or trying to make them happy. These are now things that I do for myself. That way I help free others to take responsibility for their own happiness.

Of course, I do feel the darkness of storm clouds amidst the brilliant sunshine of my days. Overcast days are part of my condition as a human being, part of being alive, part of this wonderful world.

It is a privilege to be alive.

I remember my mother with warmth and great pride. She was a woman that brought fun into my life. Yes, as well as pain and tears. But her mischievous fun was totally endearing. Her struggle to overcome her own pain was inspiring. I thank her for giving me the gift of living life to the full. I thank her for our extraordinary relationship and a profession that keeps me independent giving me constant joy and keeping me fit into my old age. Not perhaps a maternal mother but a charismatic highly intelligent emotional and dramatic person. She taught me how to survive.

The empire is shrinking. My dream and biggest desire is to build it up again. I wish it to be known that I am the only person still training the Lotte Berk technique in the authentic and original form that Lotte designed. It was her wish that I should continue her training. I am fulfilling this wish and my teacher training diploma programme is ongoing.

POMONA BOOKS

Pomona is a wholly independent publisher dedicated to bringing before the public the work of prodigiously talented writers. Our books can be purchased on-line at:

www.pomonauk.com

Pomona backlist